SURREY

THE SURREY DOMESDAY

ALECTO HISTORICAL EDITIONS
LONDON
1989

ISBN for Surrey volumes: 0 948459 45 x
ISBN for this volume: 1 871118 08 5

Printed in England

ALECTO HISTORICAL EDITIONS
46 Kelso Place, London W8 5QG, England

CONTENTS

PREFACE

THIS is the eleventh volume of the Alecto County Edition of Domesday Book to be published. Although Surrey comes third in the order of counties in Great Domesday Book, the spacing and style of the main scribe's writing show that its folios were written about one third of the way through the programme in which the thirty counties were inscribed.

In the manuscript, a single gathering of seven folios constitutes the section for Surrey, and taken overall the columns present an attractive, well-ordered uniformity. However, it soon becomes evident that the scribe had considerable difficulties with certain information which came in late. The odd folio 33 is a blank half-sheet on to which a small strip of parchment bearing five extra entries has been mounted. This anomalous leaf has been inserted at the appropriate position in the chapter devoted to the lands of the Abbey of Chertsey, though it bisects the entry for Chobham between folios 32v and 34. There are also several instances where entire passages have been erased or have had to be added in the margin, especially towards the end. On the final folio 36v the scribe wrote the first column with the usual spacing between the lines, but then realized that there was not enough room for the remainder of the text if he were to complete the county on this last page of the gathering. He therefore condensed the second column by reducing the size and spacing of his script and, in the event, just succeeded in concluding the section for Surrey in two extra lines along the bottom of the page.

The original northern boundary of Surrey was the river Thames, but since 1889 the county has continued to lose territory from that direction with the growth of London, the last important changes taking place with the establishment of Greater London in 1965. At the same time, however, because Middlesex was abolished, Surrey gained the region around Staines and Sunbury. The only change made on the occasion of the restructuring of the counties in 1974 (not normally noticed in this edition) was the loss of the Gatwick Airport complex to Sussex, which is not significant in this context as no Domesday settlement is recorded there.

The three volumes that constitute each part of the County Edition are designed to be mutually supportive and are separated in this way for the reader's convenience. For instance, it is desirable for the facsimile folios to be present in one book and the parallel translations in another so that both can be consulted side by side. For the same reason the key to the symbols employed in the translations for Great Domesday's marginal notes and signs (Appendix I), and the list of abbreviations found in the manuscript (Appendix II) are best incorporated in the third volume, *Domesday Book Studies*, so that they, too, can be used in conjunction with the folios of translations and facsimile to which they refer. A fourth separate element is the large-scale county map which is provided as a loose-leaf folded sheet in order to be spread out near at hand if required.

Besides the book containing the facsimile folios and the maps, the division of text into two further self-contained volumes reflects the character and scope of their contents. *Domesday Book Studies* (which is common to the entire County Edition) is a book of essays on topics concerning Domesday Book in general, while this volume contains all matter specific to the locality in question. The translations are put at the end, unusually after the indices, where they are easiest to find and where their pages can be matched with the facsimile of the manuscript by the same folio numbers without disrupting the pagination of the rest of this book.

In a project so closely bound up with local history, place-name identification will constitute a salient feature affecting all its aspects, especially in the translations, indices and maps where their occurrences must always be consistent. By chance, the present publication was first set in motion towards the end of a period when the place-names recorded in Domesday Book had come under particular scrutiny, but not always with unanimously accepted results. The only recourse was to log every mention of a name on to a card index and enter into it all dissident opinion. This organized body of raw material was then submitted to F. R. Thorn, appointed for his special knowledge of the Domesday hundreds and place-names, and who has also established their position on the map. Dr Thorn in turn wishes to acknowledge the help of his wife Caroline at every stage of indexing, mapping and writing the material for this county.

Those responsible for the making of the facsimile and for the production of the edition are noticed in the acknowledgements printed in the accompanying *Domesday Book Studies,* other than W. S. Cowell Ltd. of Ipswich who have typeset this particular volume. Special mention should also be made of Westerham Press for the complex task of setting the translations to match the Latin text of the manuscript with such success. The database for the manipulation of the place- and personal names for the Indices has been developed by James Brennan. The design and typography for this, as for the rest of the work, is by Ian Mortimer, I. M. Imprimit, London.

Our thanks are due especially to Elaine Shaughnessy who has controlled the editing of this volume overall, to Basil Harley for guiding the diverse elements through the press, to Brian Martin for overseeing production of the translation at Westerham Press, to Terry Concannon of W. S. Cowell Ltd., and also to the following for their diligence in the accomplishment of its various parts:

Bibliography: Dr David Bates, for rearranging his *Domesday Bibliography* already published; editing, Patricia Gibson.

Indices: Jenny Page for keying-in the material for the database from which both Indices are derived; Douglas Matthews for the compilation of the Index of Persons; Cyril Simsa and Elizabeth Mostyn-Owen for editing.

Translation: initial standardization, Eric Hemming, Paul Francis and Stephen Wilson; copy-preparation at Oxford University Press, George Tulloch; editing, J. D. Foy, Christine Shaw, Caroline Thorn; typesetting at Westerham Press, Clive Logsdon.

Map: assistance with the design, Tom Phillips; compilation and editing, Frank Thorn, Des Seal, Cyril Simsa; drafting, Sheila Hodson; overseeing production at Cook Hammond and Kell Ltd., Jackie Hoy.

Finally, at Alecto, for the myriad incidental activities that such a project requires, we must thank Sarah Burton, Henrietta Pearson and Emma Wells-Cole.

Ann Williams, *Editor-in-Chief*

R. W. H. Erskine, *General Editor*

The following is a list of abbreviations which are used throughout this edition. References to other publications are given in their abbreviated form if they occur in the county bibliography. The county volumes in this series which have already been published are cited in full at the end of the bibliography, as references to them are also abbreviated.

AntJ	*Antiquaries Journal*
ArchJ	*Archaeological Journal*
ASE	*Anglo-Saxon England*
BAR	British Archaeological Reports
BL	British Library
CA	*Current Archaeology*
DB	Domesday Book
EconHR	*Economic History Review*
EETS	Early English Text Society
EHR	*English Historical Review*
EPNS	English Place-Name Society
Exon	Exeter Domesday Book
GDB	Great Domesday Book
HMSO	Her Majesty's Stationery Office
JBAA	*Journal of the British Archaeological Association*
JMH	*Journal of Medieval History*
LDB	Little Domesday Book
MA	*Medieval Archaeology*
MS, MSS	Manuscript(s)
MS	*Mediaeval Studies*
NGR	National Grid Reference
N&Q	*Notes and Queries*
PBA	*Proceedings of the British Academy*
PRO	Public Record Office
TRHS	*Transactions of the Royal Historical Society*
VCH	*The Victoria Histories of the Counties of England*

INTRODUCTION

AN INTRODUCTION TO THE SURREY DOMESDAY

JOHN BLAIR

SMALL and rather nondescript, surrounded by areas with more strongly marked characteristics, deficient in great families, dominated and now invaded by London, Surrey has rarely commended itself to local historians. Like the shire itself, the account of it in 1086 has often been felt to lack distinctive interest and appeal. 'The Domesday Survey for the county of Surrey offers no very important or curious features, and reveals, I believe, no customs or tenures peculiar to Surrey', wrote H. E. Malden in 1886; while in 1902 J. H. Round judged it 'neither long nor of special interest'.[1]

Such verdicts, if not wholly unjust, ignore the fact that Surrey's very character as a 'border zone' gives it a certain interest of its own. The manorial structure and field-systems of medieval Surrey have tended to elude categorization: most of their attributes can be matched in Kent, Sussex, East Anglia or the Midlands, yet as a whole they will not square neatly with any of the familiar models. For the historian of English regions Surrey serves as a mirror, reflecting back the characteristics of better-known shires and revealing elements common to seemingly contrasting zones. The particular problems of interpreting the Domesday evidence for settlement in the Surrey Weald serve to highlight both the limitations of the record, and the potential for elucidating it by reference to other sources.

The Surrey folios were consulted as an historical source as early as 1377, when the Abbot of Chertsey's men at Chobham, Thorpe, Frimley and Egham bought an exemplification on the romantic but mistaken belief that it would attest their 'ancient liberties'.[2] John Aubrey, whose *Perambulation* of 1673 is the first major work devoted entirely to Surrey, only had a few notes from Domesday Book 'out of an old Manuscript in the hands of the parish-clerke of Woking'.[3] A century later, however, Owen Manning made a notable advance in Domesday studies by commissioning an engraved facsimile of the Surrey folios, the first of its kind and remarkably accurate. Engraved in 1773, Manning's plates were published in 1804 as part of his posthumous *History and Antiquities of the County of Surrey*, completed by William Bray. Bray wrote of Manning's enterprise: 'He had formed a plan, differing in one respect from that of any preceding Writer on such subjects. He began with the *Terra Regis* in Domesday . . . ; and, after illustrating it by a Commentary, he intended to deduce the History of those particular estates to modern times. He had himself drawn a map of all the places in the County mentioned in that venerable Record . . . , and he had caused to be engraved on copper a *fac simile* of the whole of it which relates to this County . . . . This is the first instance of the kind in point of time as to execution, though preceded by the Copy in Dr *Nash's* Collections for *Worcestershire*, in point of publication'.[4]

Modern scholarship on Domesday Surrey was initiated by H. E. Malden, who read a paper on the subject at the 1886 centenary.[5] Of more lasting value are his numerous contributions to *Surrey Archaeological Collections* over the next thirty years, several of which use Domesday data to interpret local topography and thus foreshadow interests of the current generation. The Surrey folios were translated by Malden, and introduced by J. H. Round, for the first volume of the *Victoria History of the County of Surrey* (1902).[6] Malden and Round laid foundations for the ever-growing volume of topographical and archaeological studies which have tried to interpret

[1] Malden, 'Domesday Survey of Surrey', 459; Round, 'Introduction', *VCH Surrey*, i (1902), 275.

[2] R. Faith, 'The "Great Rumour" of 1377 and Peasant Ideology', *The English Rising of 1381*, eds. T. H. Aston and R. H. Hilton (Cambridge, 1984), 43–73.

[3] Oxford, Bodleian Library, MS Aubrey 4, f.162.

[4] Manning and Bray, *History and Antiquities of the County of Surrey*, i. p.v.

[5] Malden, 'Domesday Survey of Surrey'.

[6] *VCH Surrey*, i. 275–328.

individual Domesday entries. Among recent general works which set the 1086 data in context, Peter Brandon's *History of Surrey* (1977) and the Surrey Archaeological Society's *Archaeology of Surrey to 1540* (eds. J. and D. G. Bird, 1987) especially deserve mention. The usual thorough analysis in the *Domesday Geography* series appeared in 1962.[1] In press at the time of writing is the present author's *Landholding, Church and Settlement in Early Medieval Surrey* (Surrey Archaeological Society Research Volume), which makes extensive use of Domesday evidence in its discussion of landscape, settlement and tenurial organization in Anglo-Saxon and Anglo-Norman Surrey.

Boundaries

South-eastern England was not one of those regions where under-exploitation of the landscape allowed major boundaries to remain vague into the twelfth century: there is every reason to think that Anglo-Saxon Surrey and early Victorian Surrey were more or less identical. Even the southern boundary, running through the lightly settled Weald, was a firm, clear line dividing the pig-pastures of the men of Surrey from those of the men of Sussex. Some entries which have been held to imply boundary changes have probably been misidentified. *Lodesorde*[2] is less likely to be Lodsworth near Midhurst (Sussex) than Lollesworth in West Horsley parish; while it is far from certain that the tiny half-hide manor of *Orde*[3] should be identified as Worth (Sussex) with its massive eleventh-century church.

The small number of links with neighbouring shires recorded in 1086 should be regarded not as evidence for unstable boundaries, but rather as traces of archaic outliers surviving from earlier times, like detached portions of parishes on modern maps. A hide in Wotton Hundred attached to Compton (near Chichester, Sussex)[4] may be a relic of trans-Weald contact centuries earlier.[5] The hide in Hampshire among the endowments of the minster church at Farnham,[6] on the Hampshire-Surrey border, can be explained by reference to the foundation of the minster in the 680s by a West Saxon king.[7] Two sulungs in Kent were attached to Merton, and woodland in Kent to Wallington:[8] links which probably reflect the complex earlier history of the eastern boundary. Anglo-Saxon Surrey seems to have gained territory at the expense of the westernmost Kentish lathe, and even in the late tenth century the district east of Wallington was dominated by Kentish interests.[9]

In 1888 several parishes in north-eastern Surrey were absorbed into the new county of London.[10] Later changes have deprived Surrey of the area covered by Brixton, Kingston and Wallington Hundreds, and given it the area around Staines (of which it may, ironically, have been the 'southern region' in the sixth or seventh century).[11] Local historians have generally, however, observed the sensible practice of ignoring these changes and defining Surrey according to its historic boundaries.

The Survey

Circuit I, the south-eastern Domesday circuit, comprised Kent, Sussex, Surrey, Hampshire and Berkshire.[12] Like all the circuits it is distinguished by a broad internal consistency of definition and terminology, common to these counties and more conspicuous than differences between them: churches are always listed rather than priests, for instance, and woodland is always measured in swine-renders rather than in leagues. On the whole Surrey is more straightforward

[1] Darby and Campbell (eds.), *Domesday Geography*, 364–405.
[2] GDB 36v. [3] GDB 34v. [4] GDB 34.
[5] See p.6 below. [6] GDB 31.
[7] P. H. Sawyer (ed.), *Anglo-Saxon Charters: An Annotated List and Bibliography*, R. Hist. Soc. Guides and Handbooks, 8 (London, 1968) (henceforward cited by number preceded by S.), S.235.
[8] GDB 30.
[9] J. Blair, *Landholding, Church and Settlement in Early Medieval Surrey*, Surrey Archaeol. Soc. Research Vol. (forthcoming), Ch. 1.
[10] *VCH Surrey*, i. 431. [11] See pp.6–7 below.
[12] For the division of the country into seven circuits, each visited by a specific group of commissioners, see H. R. Loyn, 'A General Introduction to Domesday Book', *Domesday Book Studies*, eds. A. Williams and R. W. H. Erskine (London, 1987), 3–7.

and more lacking in obvious local variation than the other four counties. Yet variations are to be found, both between Surrey and the rest of the circuit and between hundreds within the shire, which must affect our interpretation of the data and our view of their reliability. It will be useful here to consider in turn some major categories of information: hundredal designation, hides, ploughlands, plough-teams, population, values, woodland, churches. The data for other resources are unexceptional and relatively slight, and are discussed below in relation to the topography and economy of eleventh-century Surrey.

Manors in Surrey are, as always in Great Domesday, grouped by tenant-in-chief. In some counties each tenant's lands are arranged according to a consistent hundredal order, betokening the earlier stage of the inquiry at which the data were arranged by hundreds. This does not apply to Surrey,[1] where the very recording of hundreds is distinctly slipshod. Sometimes a hundredal heading is omitted (thus assigning a group of manors to the wrong hundred), or inserted in the wrong place (as on f.35v, where the heading 'in Wotton Hundred' appears after Ockley instead of before it). The hundredal stage of the inquiry must have been suppressed more thoroughly in the penultimate draft of the Surrey return than in some others, though, as we shall see,[2] it was not suppressed completely.

In Circuit I, Surrey included, the data for assessments to the geld are unusually good: only here are hidages consistently recorded both for TRE and for TRW. Surrey is therefore a good county in which to study the late Anglo-Saxon system and its modification after the Conquest. It is also one of those shires in which some writers have recognized a structure of five-hide units. Until recently, Round observed in 1902, 'it was not known that these figures represented a vast system of artificial assessment, based on what is now termed the five-hide unit, and practically unconnected with actual area or value . . . Croydon and Mortlake were assessed at 80 hides each, and Farnham at 60 . . . Merstham, Cheam and Coulsdon are examples of a 20 hides assessment, Petersham stood at 10, and Mickleham, Rodsell and Walworth at 5 hides each'.[3] This view is endorsed by Darby and Campbell's *Domesday Geography*, which notes that 'in 1066 the number of villages assessed at 5 hides, or at a multiple of 5, amounted to 52 out of a total of 142'.[4]

The existence of these symmetrical features is not in doubt, but the assumption that they represent a simple, once-for-all division into five-hide units may lack historical perspective. The principle of hidage assessment was ancient, and by 1066 it had been developing over at least four centuries. Round-figure assessments occur in the earliest Surrey charters: 300 hides at Chertsey (672–4), sixty at Farnham (685–7), twenty-eight, twenty and another twenty at Battersea (693), twenty at Woking (757–96).[5] Four of the eight Surrey manors described in reliable charters between 974 and 1005 are stated to be of twenty hides, and three, possibly all four of these had the same assessments TRE.[6] A 'basic' unit of twenty hides might as convincingly be postulated as one of five hides. Symmetrical hidation originated in the formative stages of English society, not with the military needs of late Anglo-Saxon kings.

The drastic reduction in the hidage, and thus the tax burden, of many Surrey manors between 1066 and 1086 has often been noted.[7] The fluctuations have usually been considered arbitrary and mysterious, especially since there is no correlation between reductions in hidation and reductions in value. Recently, however, a pattern has been discerned by S. P. J. Harvey, who points out that 'concessions were confined to the manors kept in hand by tenants-in chief and others who held of the king directly . . . . All landholders, great or small . . . , experienced reductions in the assessment of manors in which no subtenant was placed'. Some landlords (the Count of Mortain, Abbey of Saint-Wandrille, Battle Abbey) had their assessments abolished completely; others (such as the Count and Countess of Boulogne, St Peter's of Winchester, and Chertsey Abbey) gained huge rebates; while Richard fitzGilbert, exceptionally, enjoyed large

[1] See P. H. Sawyer, 'The "Original Returns" and Domesday Book', *EHR* 70 (1955), 180.

[2] See p.5 below.

[3] *VCH Surrey*, i. 276. In this edition Merstham is assumed to include South Merstham; Rodsell is spelt Rodsall on modern maps.

[4] Darby and Campbell (eds.), *Domesday Geography*, 373.

[5] Sawyer (ed.), S.1165, S.235, S.1248, S.144.

[6] Ibid. S.528 (Merstham); S.551/747 (Merton); S.1447 (Send); S.911 (Esher).

[7] For example, *VCH Surrey*, i. 276; Darby and Campbell (eds.), *Domesday Geography*, 372–4.

reductions on both his demesne and his tenanted manors.[1] Thus the reductions seem to betoken a general fiscal leniency towards demesnes, not necessarily related to their productivity.

Despite recent scholarship, there is still some scope for speculation on the 'dreary old question . . . what was the hide?'[2] Terminology regarding hides in the Surrey Domesday is variable, and not always wholly clear.[3] It is not inherently impossible that some hides, as originally defined, had retained their topographical and agrarian identity, and there are hints that for the compiler of Domesday a hide in terms of the TRE geld burden might sometimes still be a hide in a more physical sense. For most of the one-hide and two-hide units which appear as manors in their own right no hidation is given, as if the statement '*x* holds *y* hides' implies automatically that 'it was assessed at (*se defendit pro*) *y* hides TRE'.[4] Where a TRE hidage is indeed stated in such entries, it invariably corresponds with the number of hides that the holding is said to contain: thus 'these 2 hides were assessed at 2 hides TRE; now at half a hide'.[5] Sometimes we are told the name of a manor, its TRE hidation, and then that a certain whole number 'of these hides' have since been alienated.[6] This kind of language would make no sense unless a tract which had gelded at one hide before the Conquest was normally a stable entity and likely to remain so. This is not to deny that by 1086 the hides of the old assessment were fiscal units which had long ceased to reflect productive acreage; it is merely to suggest that they were not *purely* fiscal, but had occasionally retained some distinctness in the fabric of land tenure or rural society.

In contrast to hides, the information on ploughlands and plough-teams in the Surrey Domesday has little of general interest to offer. The data, especially for ploughlands, are vitiated by numerous blanks, and they do not greatly advance the vexed question of how the phrase 'there is land for *x* ploughs' should be interpreted. As often, the lack of correlation between teams and ploughlands is striking, with understocking on about a third of the manors for which ploughlands are recorded, and overstocking on about two-fifths. Overstocking is especially marked in the hundred of Woking, with totals of 136½ teams to 99½ ploughlands.[7]

The inhabitants of Domesday Surrey are classified according to the usual categories of villan, bordar, cottar and slave. There is little deviation from the norm, the only exceptional tenant (apart from some burgesses) being a solitary 'forester' at Walton-on-Thames.[8] There is a relatively high proportion of slaves compared with Kent and Sussex, though notably few on monastic and chapter lands.[9] Surrey is one of those counties in which the usage of *bordarius* and *cotarius* is of some interest. The problem was succinctly summed up by Malden: 'One tenure or the other would seem to prevail according to local custom, for they only occur once together on the same manor, and very seldom in the same hundred. They both occur with *villani* and with *servi*. There are three hundreds, Godalming, Wallington, and Elmbridge, where the *cotarii* are nearly universal, to the exclusion of *bordarii*. In the others the *bordarii* are nearly or quite universal, to the exclusion of the *cotarii*. In Godalming hundred there are *cotarii*, and no *bordarii* except at Godalming itself, where there are *bordarii* on the part of the manor which is in royal demesne, an exception which may be compared with the state of things at Wallington. In Wallington hundred there are many *cotarii*, and *bordarii* at only two places, at Wallington on King William's land and at Croydon on the Archbishop's. In Elmbridge hundred there are *cotarii*, and no *bordarii* except one *bordarius* at Weybridge and some at East Moulsey. In Blackheath hundred there are *cotarii* at Bramley, along the borders of Godalming hundred where *cotarii* abound, and in Brixton hundred there are *cotarii* at Tooting on the borders of Wallington hundred. In the rest of these and in the other hundreds there are *bordarii* and no *cotarii*. The three "cotarian" hundreds are not adjacent, they are not on some peculiar soil which might imply some peculiar form of industry or tenure, they are not in the possession of the same people. Indeed they represent all the soils of Surrey. Godalming, the Lower Greensand bordering the Weald and the Chalk;

[1] S. P. J. Harvey, 'Taxation and the Economy', *Domesday Studies*, ed. J. C. Holt (Woodbridge, 1987), 257–9.
[2] F. W. Maitland, *Domesday Book and Beyond* (Cambridge, 1897), 357.
[3] Cf. comments in Darby and Campbell (eds.), *Domesday Geography*, 371–2.
[4] For example, Tooting (?Graveney) (f.33).
[5] Hamo the sheriff's holding (f.33).
[6] For example, Cuddington (f.31v).
[7] Darby and Campbell (eds.), *Domesday Geography*, 375.
[8] GDB 36.
[9] Malden, 'Domesday Survey of Surrey', 469.

Elmbridge, the Bagshot Sand, London Clay and alluvium; Wallington, the Chalk and London Clay. Besides the local distribution of the two tenures, the only rule for their occurrence seems to be that there are no *cotarii* on royal demesne.'[1]

Malden's explanation in terms of 'local custom' is not supported by later sources. For example, at Godalming Domesday lists twenty-nine bordars on the royal demesne and twelve cottars on the church land.[2] By the early fourteenth century there were fourteen twelve-acre 'cotlands' on the royal demesne and another twelve on the glebe, and it is hard to believe that the smallholders on these two interlocking manors were not already of like kind in 1086.[3] The real explanation, and the real interest, of the differences is that they provide a glimpse of the 'original returns' to the survey. Some compilers of hundredal returns used *bordarius*, others *cotarius*. Returns from royal demesne were made separately and always used *bordarius*, while occasional discrepancies suggest that the terminology of other fief-based returns (such as the Archbishop of Canterbury's for Croydon) was not completely ironed out at the next stage.

Values are normally given for TRE, 'afterwards' and 'now', though again there are some gaps.[4] Many manors show a dramatic fluctuation, falling to well under half the TRE value at 'afterwards', but then recovering or rising even higher by 1086. The inference, often made, that these patterns reflect economic disruption in the aftermath of the Conquest seems reasonable enough, though it is doubtful if the path of William's army around London can really be traced by means of reduced manorial values.[5]

The data for woodland in the Surrey Domesday are copious, but in practice almost unusable.[6] The normal formula is 'woodland for *x* pigs' or 'woodland for *x* pigs as pannage'. This does not denote the number of pigs that the wood could support, but the number of pigs payable to the lord by his tenants for the use of the wood, normally a proportion of their total herds. Unfortunately for the Domesday geographer, this proportion varied even within Surrey: one pig in ten is mentioned at Battersea and Streatham, but one in seven at Old Malden and Titsey.[7] Since these are the only manors where proportions are stated, there is no common multiplier to provide even relative indications of the amount of woodland attached to each manor. Worse still, later sources show that Surrey wood-pastures often lay many miles distant from their present manors,[8] thus precluding the mapping of swine-renders without recourse to external evidence.

Churches are mentioned frequently. The normal formula in all the Circuit I counties is 'There is a church' (*Est ibi aecclesia*).[9] In Kent, independent sources show that only about half the churches standing in 1086 were noted by the Domesday commissioners,[10] and at first sight this seems important comparative evidence for assessing the value of the Surrey data. Certainly there are demonstrable omissions from the Surrey list,[11] and it is arguable that there were many more omissions which cannot be demonstrated. None the less, there are some grounds for thinking that in this respect the quality of data is not consistent within the circuit, and that the record of churches is considerably better for Surrey than for Kent.[12] Among a total of 235 separately listed properties in Surrey, sixty-one (or 26 per cent) are credited with churches. The incidence of churches is weighted heavily towards the more valuable and populous estates, a large majority of which are stated to have them. Here there is a clear contrast with Kent, where churches are

[1] Malden, 'Domesday Survey of Surrey', 469–70; however, Malden has ascribed *cotarii* to Tooting in error. In this edition Elmbridge Hundred is 'Elmbridge'; Moulsey is spelt Molesey on modern maps.

[2] GDB 30v.

[3] Blair, *Early Medieval Surrey*, Ch. 3; P. Woods, 'The Parsonage, or Rectory Manor of Godalming, and a Fourteenth-Century Custumal Thereof', *Surrey Archaeol. Collections* 22 (1909), 115–36; P. Woods, 'On a Fourteenth-Century Rental of the Principal Manor of Godalming; with Some Remarks on Cotholders', *Surrey Archaeol. Collections* 23 (1910), 91–107.

[4] See fuller discussion in Darby and Campbell (eds.), *Domesday Geography*, 382–4.

[5] Cf. Round, *VCH Surrey*, i. 278–9.

[6] See fuller discussion in Darby and Campbell (eds.), *Domesday Geography*, 386–9.

[7] GDB 32, 34v, 35, 36v.

[8] See pp.10–11 below.

[9] The most detailed analysis of terminology is in D. H. Gifford, 'The Parish in Domesday Book' (unpubl. Ph.D. thesis, London Univ., 1952), 91–6.

[10] R. Lennard, *Rural England 1086–1135* (Oxford, 1959), 293–4; T. Tatton-Brown, 'The Churches of Canterbury Diocese in the Eleventh Century', *Minsters and Parish Churches: the Local Church in Transition, 950–1200*, ed. J. Blair, Oxford Univ. Committee for Archaeology Monograph 17 (1988), 105–18.

[11] Lingfield and Sanderstead; probably Wotton, Thursley and Godstone; perhaps Thorncroft and Bletchingley.

[12] Evidence set out in Blair, *Early Medieval Surrey*, Ch. 5.

unmentioned on numerous large estates of a kind that would normally have them in the Surrey Domesday. If in Surrey, as in Kent, no more than some 50 per cent of existing churches had been recorded, so clear and credible a pattern could scarcely have emerged. The later Surrey evidence seems equally incompatible with gross deficiencies in 1086: well over half of the parish churches which existed by *c.*1200 appear in Domesday Book, and many of the remainder are interpretable as post-Domesday foundations. Imperfect though their record undoubtedly was, it seems a fair conclusion that the commissioners listed a large majority of the churches standing in Surrey in 1086.

The Origins of the Shire

Anglo-Saxon Surrey was never a separate kingdom; nor, until the ninth century, was it even a stable element within a kingdom.[1] As early as 568, when Ceawlin of Wessex 'fought against Æthelberht and drove him in flight into Kent',[2] it appears as frontier territory buffeted between the southern English rulers. Especially revealing of its political and territorial origins are two seemingly contradictory facts: on the one hand the economic unity of Kent, Sussex and Surrey, the three Wealden counties; and on the other the name Surrey, which seems to imply that it was once part of some larger entity of which the rest lay north of the Thames. As the Surrey problem well illustrates, the elements in the melting-pot from which Anglo-Saxon kingdoms were formed are hard to define simply.

The great woodland common of the Weald stamps on the three shires of Kent, Sussex and Surrey a broad geographical uniformity. All around it, near the coast and in the Thames Valley, were early-settled communities which looked inland to the wood-pasture of the Weald. It was an extended, transhumant economy, with herds of swine driven down long, straight droveways to summer pastures deep in the woodland. There is thus an obvious sense in which Kent, Sussex and about two-thirds of Surrey divide naturally into broad swathes of land radiating out of the Weald. By the eighth century some of these swathes had acquired an administrative and economic identity. The 'pre-hundredal' divisions of Kent and Sussex survived into the high Middle Ages as lathes and rapes; in Surrey, where the early pattern has been more heavily obscured, it is still possible to identify comparable early territories comprising the central and eastern thirds of the shire.[3] Cemetery and place-name evidence, implying trans-Weald contact along the Roman iron-ways in the early Anglo-Saxon period, reinforces the apparent unity of Sussex and Surrey: thus it has been argued that the *Poling* names scattered along the line of Stane Street from Poling in Sussex to Pallinghurst and Pollingfold in Surrey 'strongly suggest that the coastal villages of Felpham and Poling had a group of dependent hamlets stretching right across the Weald beyond the borders of the South Saxon kingdom'.[4]

Against this must be set the obvious fact that a major line of Saxon advance was along the Thames. The earliest colonization of northern Surrey seems to have followed the Wey, Mole and Wandle valleys, especially the Wandle with its group of large cemeteries in the Croydon-Mitcham area. This is not, of course, incompatible with advance from the south, but it suggests a pattern in which the Thames acted less as a barrier between ethnic groups than as an artery from which one folk could infiltrate the land on either side. The name Surrey—*suthre ge*, 'the southern province'—has long drawn historians to a view summed up by Gover, Mawer and Stenton in 1934: 'If the name Surrey is parallel to the names Suffolk and Eastry, it can hardly have meant anything else than the southern province of the original Middle Saxons. The early history of this

[1] This section summarizes arguments set out more fully in Blair, *Early Medieval Surrey*, Introduction; J. Blair, 'Frithuwold's Kingdom and the Origins of Surrey', *The Origins of Anglo-Saxon Kingdoms*, ed. S. Bassett (Leicester, forthcoming).

[2] *Anglo-Saxon Chronicle* (abbr. *ASC*), 568: C. Plummer, *Two of the Saxon Chronicles Parallel* (Oxford, 1892–9), i. 19 (text); D. Whitelock *et al.* (eds.), *The Anglo-Saxon Chronicle: A Revised Translation* (London, 1961), 12 (translation).

[3] Blair, *Early Medieval Surrey*, Ch. 1.

[4] G. J. Copley, 'Stane Street in the Dark Ages', *Sussex Archaeol. Collections* 89 (1950), 102.

people is extremely obscure. London and presumably the whole of Middlesex had come to form part of the East Saxon kingdom before the end of the sixth century, and there is no record of any Middle Saxon dynasty. On the other hand, it is hard to believe that a people bearing such a name as *Middle Seaxe*, strictly analogous in form to *Suth Seaxe* or *Middel Enge*, were originally confined within the narrow limits of the modern Middlesex . . . . A territory comprising both Middlesex and Surrey would be large enough to support one of the smaller peoples of the sixth century, and its division into two parts by the Thames would be exactly parallel to the recorded division of the early Mercians into two provinces separated by the Trent.'[1]

One approach to this problem is to note that the Kentish *-ge* names, Eastry, Sturry and Wye, denoted individual lathes or hundreds and thus areas much smaller than Surrey. Could the original Surrey have been equally small? For Bede it was not a *provincia* but merely a *regio*, a word which he often uses for territories of the kind of order of magnitude of a Kentish lathe.[2] It may be relevant here that the westernmost third of Surrey showed a totally different kind of territorial geography from the rest: rather than looking towards the Weald, it comprised two early *regiones*, centred on the royal manors of Woking and Godalming, which were comparable to the territories of Sonning and Reading extending north-westwards up the Thames.[3] The Woking and Godalming territories, divorced from the rest of the later shire, might make more sense as the 'southern province' of an early Thames Valley kingdom.

In this context may be considered the one piece of solid evidence for the political origins of Surrey: the charter, dating between 672 and 674, by which 'Frithuwold of the province of the men of Surrey, sub-king of Wulfhere king of Mercia', grants land by the Thames to Chertsey Abbey. The north-west boundary of this estate was 'the next province which is called Sonning'; the east boundary was 'the ancient ditch, that is *Fullingadic*'. The latter can be identified as an earthwork which ran southwards from the Thames at Weybridge, dividing the Woking and Godalming territories to its west from the 'Weald-orientated' zones of Surrey to its east.[4] Apparently Frithuwold was not a native king of Surrey, but a great Mercian nobleman and a client of the overlord Wulfhere; it is arguable that he ruled a large sub-kingdom on the south-eastern fringe of Mercia which extended down the valley of the Thames from Buckinghamshire, between Mercia proper and the Middle Saxons, and which thus included the Reading and Sonning *regiones*.[5] This hypothesis introduces a political entity of which Surrey, or part of Surrey, could have been the *suthre ge*.

Both Frithuwold's realm and the Middle Saxon kingdom may have been, like the Middle Angles, relatively late creations: amalgams of tribal territories only welded together under seventh-century Mercian overlordship.[6] In the last analysis it seems most convincing to identify the area west of *Fullingadic*, which was economically of a piece with the Thames Valley territories, as the original Surrey: it could then be seen as the southern half of a lost sixth-century chiefdom of which the remainder would have been the Staines *regio* on the north side of the Thames.

The eastwards enlargement of Surrey at the expense of Kent can apparently be dated closely. The monastery at Chertsey had been founded *c.*666 under King Egbert of Kent, as is explicitly stated in Frithuwold's charter granted between 672 and 674.[7] By the latter date the whole of medieval Surrey (or at any rate its frontier along the Thames) seems to have been in Frithuwold's hands, for the charter also mentions land opposite the port of London; Bermondsey Minster was founded a few years later, evidently in the context of patronage by Frithuwold's family.[8] Thus it seems not unlikely that Frithuwold had himself played a major part in the Mercian advance south of the Thames, and had been rewarded with some of the conquered land. Surrey is not identifiable in the late seventh-century Tribal Hidage, unless we locate there the unintelligible

[1] Gover *et al.* (eds.), *Place-Names of Surrey*, pp.xiv–xv.
[2] See J. Campbell, *Essays in Anglo-Saxon History* (London, 1986), 86–7.
[3] Blair, 'Frithuwold's Kingdom'.
[4] Blair, *Early Medieval Surrey*, Ch. 1.
[5] Blair, 'Frithuwold's Kingdom'.
[6] Cf. papers by Bailey, Blair and Dumville in *Origins of Anglo-Saxon Kingdoms*, ed. Bassett.
[7] Sawyer (ed.), S.1165.
[8] See p.14 below.

Noxgaga and *Ohtgaga*, or follow J. C. Russell's conjecture that *Hendrica* and *Unecungga* are scribal perversions of *Sudrica* and *Suningga*.[1] The latter suggestion, if correct, would give Surrey 3,500 hides, which may be compared with the 2,400 hides assessed to Eashing and Southwark in the Burghal Hidage, and with the 2,000 hides for which the county was assessed in 1086.[2]

By the late 680s Cædwalla had decisively turned the power-balance south of the Thames in favour of Wessex, and his Farnham charter of between 685 and 688 shows him master of south-western Surrey.[3] It is certain that he and his successor Ine both exercised authority in Surrey, if perhaps uneasily and intermittently,[4] and a papal privilege of between 708 and 715 locates the Surrey monasteries of Bermondsey and Woking *in provincia West Saxonum*.[5] We next hear of Surrey under the Mercian overlordship of Offa, whose confirmation of a grant to Woking Church was issued from a royal vill *in regione Suthregeona*.[6] From the victory of Egbert of Wessex in 825, when the men of Surrey, Kent, Sussex and Essex submitted to him 'because they had been wrongly forced away from (allegiance to) his kinsmen',[7] Surrey was decisively part of Wessex. It was probably during the next few decades that it finally gained coherence as a West Saxon shire, with boundaries much as they remained until modern times.

During much of the Anglo-Saxon period, local government operated from 'royal vills': regional manor-houses or palaces, only intermittently visited by the itinerating kings and their courts but with permanent staffs of administrative officials. Even in the more urbanized tenth and eleventh centuries the royal vills remained important as centres of justice and tax-collection, and many of the new towns were founded in close proximity to them. The 'royal vill called *Freoricburna* in the region of Surrey' where kings issued charters in the late eighth and early ninth centuries may be identical with Kingston upon Thames, the scene of a church council in 838 and an important royal centre thereafter.[8] King Alfred's will (between 879 and 888) mentions other royal estates at Eashing, Godalming, Guildford, Leatherhead and Thunderfield.[9] In 1066 the principal royal vills were (in order of value) Godalming, Kingston upon Thames, Ewell, Wallington, Woking and Stoke (in Guildford).[10] Eashing and Thunderfield had disappeared from view; the Leatherhead complex, which may have been substantial in Alfred's time, had been dismembered leaving only a residue of land at Ewell.[11]

Two Surrey places, Eashing and Southwark, appear in the early tenth-century list of fortress-towns known as the Burghal Hidage.[12] The first of these had been established on the complex of royal lands in the Wey valley, represented by Eashing and Guildford in King Alfred's will and by Stoke (in Guildford) in Domesday Book. The site of the Eashing *burh* is identifiable as a natural promontory between two small valleys, cut off by a bank and ditch.[13] This location was too restricted and isolated for urban growth; during the tenth century it was replaced by a new fortified town at Guildford, where coins were minted between 975 and the Conquest.[14] The role of Southwark (*Suthringa geweorche*, 'the fort of the men of Surrey', or *Suth geweorche*, 'the south fort')[15] was rather different: as the later version of its name implies, it formed a bulwark at the southern end of London Bridge guarding the approach to London. A mint existed there under Æthelræd II, and the *burh* figured prominently in the Danish raids of the late tenth and early eleventh centuries.[16] Southwark was blockaded by Earl Godwine's ships during the crisis of 1052, and burnt by William in the course of his encirclement of London after the Battle of Hastings.

1 J. C. Russell, 'The Tribal Hidage', *Traditio*, 5 (1947), 197.

2 *VCH Surrey*, i. 276–7. This misquotes the Burghal Hidage figures, for which a preferred version (1,800 hides to Southwark, 600 hides to Eashing) is given by D. Hill, 'The Burghal Hidage: the Establishment of a Text', *MA* 13 (1969), 86–7.

3 Sawyer (ed.), S.235.

4 Cf. F. M. Stenton, *Anglo-Saxon England* (3rd edn., Oxford, 1971), 72–3.

5 W. de G. Birch, *Cartularium Saxonicum: A Collection of Charters Relating to Anglo-Saxon History* (London, 1885–99; repr. 1964), no. 133.

6 Sawyer (ed.), S.144.

7 *ASC* 823 (= 825): Plummer, *Two of the Saxon Chronicles*, i. 60 (text); Whitelock *et al.* (eds.), *Anglo-Saxon Chronicle*, 40 (translation).

8 Sawyer (ed.), S.144, S.280; Birch, *Cartularium Saxonicum*, no. 421.

9 Sawyer (ed.), S.1507.

10 GDB 30–30v.

11 Blair, *Early Medieval Surrey*, Ch. 1.

12 Hill, 'Burghal Hidage'.

13 F. Aldsworth and D. Hill, 'The Burghal Hidage: Eashing', *Surrey Archaeol. Collections* 68 (1971), 198–201.

14 D. Hill, *An Atlas of Anglo-Saxon England* (Oxford, 1981), map 224; J. and D. G. Bird (eds.), *The Archaeology of Surrey to 1540*, Surrey Archaeol. Soc. (Guildford, 1987), 208–9.

15 Gover *et al.* (eds.), *Place-Names of Surrey*, 29–30.

16 See D. J. Johnson, *Southwark and the City* (Oxford, 1969), Chs. 1–2; *VCH Surrey*, iv (1967), 125–6. M. Biddle and D. M. Hudson, *The Future of London's Past* (Worcester, 1973), fig. 9, shows the possible perimeter of the *burh*.

The Landscape of Domesday Surrey

Surrey, in Peter Brandon's words, 'recalls to mind not one landscape but a mosaic of four—the still densely wooded Weald; the wild, rough sweeps of heathland around Hindhead and Leith Hill; the Chalk upland of the North Downs; and the quiet reposeful vales which interweave the other landscapes together'.[1] Though a small county, it has always been characterized by contrasting regions, based on geological strata which run in narrow bands from east to west. The North Downs, high and broad in the east and tapering westwards into the straight, narrow ridge called the Hog's Back, form the backbone of the county. On both sides the Chalk dips below large overlying expanses of Clay: northwards in the London Basin, continuing along the dip-slope of the Downs as a broad clay vale, and southwards in the Weald, extending across Sussex to the South Downs. Along the dip-slope, a narrow but fertile strip of Reading and Thanet Beds divides the Chalk from the heavy London Clay. The scarp-slope, too, is separated from the Weald Clay by a broader band of lighter soil, the Lower Greensand Belt, which extends westwards from Kent through the Vale of Holmesdale and widens out to include most of south-western Surrey. This linear pattern is only broken in the north-west of the county, which lies on the barren, sandy soils of the Bagshot Series.

Surrey contains little good agricultural land. Both the Weald Clay and the London Clay are heavy to work, boggy and liable in their natural state to acquire a heavy oak cover. The broom-grown heaths of the Bagshot area are among the worst land in southern Britain, and even eighteenth- and nineteenth-century improvers tended to dismiss them as hopeless.[2] The Chalk and Greensand were lighter, but relatively poor in their yield. The best soils lay in narrow ribbons along the dip-slope and the scarp-slope of the Downs: by the eleventh or twelfth century the villages and field-systems strung out along these lines formed a strongly marked pattern. Geology has always dictated that the agrarian landscape of Surrey should be varied: a balance of different resources within short range of each other, rather than the great expanses of open field which characterized 'champion' England.

Naturally enough, the main lines of west-east communication have always been along the Thames and the Chalk slopes. The development of the 'North Downs trackways' is controversial, but both the main ridgeway and the line along the scarp-slope terrace probably approximate to ancient routes. Further north, an early trackway connected the villages dotted along the dip-slope. The main arteries southwards from the Thames were the rivers Wey, Mole and Wandle, though all were too small to be of much use for large-scale navigation. Stane Street, the Roman road from Chichester to London, traversed the Wealden forest and linked the more settled areas of Sussex and Surrey. The whole of the Surrey Weald is broken up by long tracks running from north to south; some may be Roman iron-ways, but most are drove-roads produced by the complex transhumance grazing systems of the earlier Middle Ages. They help to explain the persistent north-south linearity of boundaries which is so noticeable in the southern part of the county.

It is now recognized that the age of Domesday Book was an age of great change in the structure of local society: common-field agriculture was developing, nucleated settlements were forming, and township communities were growing in identity and cohesion. In some parts of England the primitive pattern had by the eleventh century been totally obliterated by the 'developed' landscape of villages and open fields, whereas in others it survived almost intact. As a broad generalization, the critical changes were most advanced in regions of intensive grain production, and most retarded in regions where the wood-pasture economy remained important.[3] The distinctive characteristic of early medieval Surrey is that it was 'transitional', embodying elements both of the 'champion' and of the 'wood-pasture' zones. As so often, these

[1] P. Brandon, *A History of Surrey* (London, 1977), 15. The following paragraphs are based on Blair, *Early Medieval Surrey*, Introduction.

[2] Cf. Brandon, *History of Surrey*, 18.

[3] See, for instance, studies in T. Rowley (ed.), *The Origins of Open Field Agriculture* (London, 1981), especially H. S. A. Fox, 'Approaches to the Adoption of the Midland System'.

characteristics are latent rather than explicit in Domesday Book: the 1086 data have to be fitted into the broad canvas supplied by wider topographical studies.[1]

The most economically developed areas were the Thames Basin and the dip-slope of the Downs. Later sources show that in most townships between a third and two-thirds of the arable was farmed in open fields. These never attained the comprehensiveness of their Midland counterparts: there is little evidence for systematic three-course rotations, and the cultivators lived side-by-side with farmers of enclosed smallholdings which may often have originated far back in the Anglo-Saxon period. These mixed arable communities were of long standing by at least the late twelfth century, and probably represent the world of the Domesday villans. The open fields with their regular tenemental structure may well have developed under the guiding hands of the last Anglo-Saxon and first Anglo-Norman landlords.

The zones in which open-field farming was most advanced were also those in which nucleated villages were most prominent. In the northern half of the county, and especially along the fertile belt on the dip-slope of the Downs, were many substantial villages with marks of formal planning. This applies most notably to villages on Chertsey Abbey manors, where the striking regularity of Effingham, Great Bookham, Chobham, Egham and Chertsey betrays the systematic intervention of one landlord.[2] But not all inhabitants of such communities lived in villages: the surrounding landscape was littered with small farmsteads which can sometimes be identified in Domesday Book, and which may often have been older than the villages themselves.[3] Place-names including elements such as *worth*, several mentioned in tenth-century charters,[4] record these farmsteads, and Domesday Book itself suggests one at Shalford where there were two brothers: 'each one had his own house, and yet they resided in 1 court (*curia*)'.[5] The classic model of interdependent peasant cultivators, living in a central village and farming the common fields around it, certainly existed in Surrey; but it never, as so often in the Midlands, became all-embracing.

These remarks apply to those parts of Surrey which supported permanent settlement from relatively early in the Anglo-Saxon period. Far different was the position on the Weald Clay and Greensands south of the line of the Downs, which were only systematically colonized between the tenth and the twelfth centuries. Here there were few regularly planned settlements or smallholders, and no open fields; the dominant impression of the sources is of constant growth and change. The interpretation of Domesday data becomes even more difficult than usual, for the format of the record is ill-suited to expressing conditions of social and economic flux. The problems are, however, worth mastering, for it is such areas that best reveal the dynamics of settlement in the age of Domesday Book.

For few parts of England is settlement history so controversial as that of the Weald. The traditional view is summed up by Round's statement of 1899 that the Weald 'was still, at the time of the Conquest, a belt of some twenty miles in width, of forest, not yet opened up, except in a few scattered spots, for human settlement'.[6] Gradually, historians have come to realize that the absence from Domesday Book of Wealden place-names is misleading, reflecting not a lack of settlement but an undeveloped estate structure: within a large estate, the data for many dispersed settlements and pasture tracts were normally lumped together under one name. F. W. Maitland, prescient as usual, recognized this in relation to Farnham as long ago as 1897: 'we certainly must not draw the inference that there was but one vill in this tract. If the bishop is tenant-in-chief of the whole hundred and has become responsible for all the geld that is levied therefrom, there is no great reason why the surveyors should trouble themselves about the vills. Thus the simple *Episcopus tenet Ferneham* may dispose of some 24,000 acres of land.'[7]

Surrey long retained a type of estate structure whereby manors in the Thames Basin or along the line of the Downs had outlying portions several miles southwards, deep in the Weald. By the

[1] For what follows, see Blair, *Early Medieval Surrey*, Chs. 2–3.

[2] Ibid. fig. 18. See also Bird and Bird (eds.), *Archaeology of Surrey*, 243–4.

[3] Blair, *Early Medieval Surrey*, Ch. 1. and fig. 15.

[4] Ibid. Ch. 2.

[5] GDB 35v.

[6] J. H. Round, 'The Settlement of the South- and East-Saxons', *The Commune of London and Other Studies* (Westminster, 1899), 3.

[7] Maitland, *Domesday Book and Beyond*, 13–14.

later Middle Ages these outliers were mostly settled farmland, but late Anglo-Saxon charters record them as pig-pastures to which swine were driven for fattening in the pannage season. Thus in the tenth or eleventh century Sutton (near Cheam) had woods with 'beds of pigs' at Horley; in 947 Merstham had dependencies at Petridge Wood, Lake and Thunderfield, all again in Horley; and between 963 and 975 a large estate at Beddington had 'land with attached woods' at *Cysledun*, Tandridge and Lake.[1] The settlement of these enclaves produced a distinctive pattern of farms and hamlets which in Kent are often identified by place-names with the suffix *-denn* (Biddenden, Tenterden, etc.). This was not a Surrey term (though the Domesday entry for Ewell does mention 'a woodland dene', *unam denam silvae*),[2] and the main local equivalents were apparently *-falod* ('fold') and *-ersc* (?'newly-broken land'). The concentration of names containing these elements in the Wealden parts of Godalming, Blackheath and Wotton Hundreds (for instance Chiddingfold, Alfold, Dunsfold, Wonersh, Haldish, Linersh)[3] suggests a phase of intensive, localized colonization which probably post-dated the tenth-century references to pig-pastures, and may well have been in full spate at the time when the Domesday survey was in progress.

The commissioners grouped the resources of such outliers, whether consisting of pasture or of colonizing peasants, under the parent manor: uncritical plotting of data according to estate centres produces the absurd result of a map showing the Surrey Weald devoid both of inhabitants and of woodland.[4] A more rational approach is to try to deduce, from the later history of each individual manor, which of its resources listed in 1086 are likely to have been Wealden. For present purposes two examples will suffice. First, the Chertsey Abbey manor of Sutton (near Cheam) is stated in Domesday Book to have two churches.[5] Only one church is recorded at Sutton thereafter; but since much of Horley had been attached to Sutton before the Conquest it seems highly likely that the other was in fact the parish church of Horley, which is recorded in Chertsey Abbey's hands in 1176.[6] A church implies a settled community, so it may be inferred that the 'beds of pigs' of the late Anglo-Saxon charters had at least been partly colonized by 1086. The second example concerns Richard of Tonbridge's manor at Chevington, which stretched southwards from the scarp-slope of the Downs to the Sussex border and included the later Wealden parish of Horne. The Domesday entry does not mention Horne, but says that one Roger holds half a hide in the manor.[7] This man might tentatively be identified as Roger d'Abernon, a frequent subtenant on Clare manors, and the likelihood is greatly strengthened by the fact that the head of the d'Abernon family in the next generation held land at Bysshe Court (i.e. *bysc*, 'bush', 'thicket') in Horne.[8] Once again, the correlation of Domesday Book with later sources reveals a hidden reference to an incipient Wealden community.

These cases illustrate not merely the dynamics of Domesday settlement, but also the dynamics of modern Domesday scholarship. Further elucidation of the settlement and landscape data will only be possible through detailed local studies. In Surrey as elsewhere, much latent information remains to be recovered, and its recovery is often within the scope of the local enthusiast.

The Social Structure of Domesday Surrey

In the eyes of King William's government, the focal points of any shire were its centre of administration and local justice: the county town and the hundredal meeting-places. The place which figures most prominently in the Surrey Domesday is Guildford, which was confirmed as the county town in 1257.[9] Leatherhead has some rival claim to be regarded as the early

[1] Sawyer (ed.), S.420/752, S.528, S.815. The pre-Conquest settlement of Lake is represented by Greatlake and Littlelake Farms on modern maps.

[2] GDB 30v.

[3] Blair, *Early Medieval Surrey*, fig. 13, and Brandon, *History of Surrey*, map p.29.

[4] Cf. the county map issued with this volume; Darby and Campbell (eds.), *Domesday Geography*, 387–9.

[5] GDB 32v.

[6] W. Holtzmann (ed.), *Papsturkunden in England*, i (Berlin, 1930), 406.

[7] GDB 34v.

[8] Blair, 'Early History of Horne: an Addendum'.

[9] M. O'Connell, *Historic Towns in Surrey*, Surrey Archaeol. Soc. Research Vol. 5 (Guildford, 1977), 29.

centre, even though Domesday Book merely mentions its church. As late as the thirteenth century the residue of Leatherhead royal manor was held for sergeanty services associated with royal justice; these included finding a bench for the county court, which according to jurors in 1259 had 'always' been held at Leatherhead.[1] It was none the less at Guildford, encircled by his large manors of Godalming, Stoke (in Guildford), Woking and Shere, that William I established his seat of shire government and principal stronghold. The great earthen motte of Guildford Castle may well date from William's reign, though both the polygonal shell keep on its summit and the surviving tower keep were added after 1100.[2]

The later medieval division of Surrey into its fourteen hundreds (Blackheath, Brixton, 'Copthorne', Effingham, 'Elmbridge', Farnham, Godalming, 'Godley', Kingston, Reigate, Tandridge, Wallington, Woking, Wotton) was fully formed by 1086: all are mentioned in Domesday Book except Farnham, which was one large manor which lacks a hundredal rubric. Although careless rubrication hampers reconstruction of the Domesday hundreds it is clear that their boundaries were essentially as later, with only trivial differences (notably Great Burgh, in Wallington Hundred, and Chessington, in Kingston, both of which were transferred to 'Copthorne' Hundred).[3]

Despite the changes in the structure and personnel of government since 1066, the king's most important officer in the shire was still the sheriff. A chance reference in the Wandsworth entry shows that an earlier sheriff, and probably the first Norman, had been Ansculf de Picquigny, father of the tenant-in-chief William fitzAnsculf.[4] Ranulph, the sheriff in 1086, appears holding a tenement in Guildford, and again as involved in a dispute with Odo of Bayeux about the minster and waterway in Southwark.[5]

Much of the king's wealth came from the king's land. In Surrey this still mostly consisted of the old royal estates and hundredal centres: Kingston upon Thames, Woking, Wallington, Godalming, Ewell-Leatherhead. A special group of manors (Reigate, Shere, Dorking, Fetcham), in the king's own hands by 1086, had belonged to Queen Edith TRE and may, like such estates elsewhere, have been assigned to the late Anglo-Saxon queens on a regular basis. The geography of these is distinctive: all except Fetcham lay in the southern half of the county, stretching deep into the Weald from the scarp-slope of the Downs. It seems likely that they represent a later stage of estate formation than the old royal estates in northern and western Surrey. Finally, the king had annexed Bermondsey, Merton and Gomshall, manors which may not originally have been royal but which had belonged to Harold before 1066.[6]

Surrey did not contain the principal seat of any earl or major baron. Rather it was dominated, and had probably long been dominated, by lay and ecclesiastical magnates based in Kent, Sussex and Hampshire. The only great religious landowner within the county was Chertsey Abbey, which retained the great estate in north-west Surrey acquired in the 670s.[7] The see of Canterbury still held its ancient estates of Croydon and Mortlake, and the see of Winchester the whole of Farnham Hundred (formerly the endowment of Farnham Minster) which it had acquired by the tenth century.[8] Apart from the members of the house of Godwine, the biggest lay landowners TRE were 'Alnod Cild' and 'Brixi Cild', almost certainly identifiable with the Kentish noblemen Æthelnoth of Canterbury and Beorhtsige.[9] Predictably, the two greatest lords in 1086 also had their centres of gravity in Kent: the king's half-brother Odo of Bayeux (listed as a tenant-in-chief even though he had been in prison for four years), and Richard of Tonbridge, founder of the honour of Clare, whose main residences were at Tonbridge (Kent) and Clare (Suffolk).[10] Odo's Surrey manors were concentrated in Blackheath Hundred, but there is no evidence that he had a castle or major estate centre in Surrey. Richard of Tonbridge, on the

[1] J. H. Harvey, '"The Mounts", Pachenesham: an Historical Note', *Proc. of the Leatherhead and District Local Hist. Soc.* 1. i (1977), 9–11.

[2] D. F. Renn, *Norman Castles in Britain* (London, 1968).

[3] GDB 36v, 32. For another view on the status of Great Burgh, see F. R. Thorn, 'Hundreds and Wapentakes', pp.20, 23 below.

[4] GDB 35v–36. [5] GDB 30, 32. [6] GDB 30–30v.

[7] GDB 32v; Sawyer (ed.), S.1165.

[8] GDB 30v–31; Sawyer (ed.), S.235; S.818.

[9] For 'Alnod', *VCH Surrey*, i. 282–3; for 'Brixi', C. A. R. Radford, 'The Church of St Mary, Stoke D'Abernon, Surrey', *ArchJ* 118 (1961), 171.

[10] GDB 31–32, 34v–35v. See Mortimer, 'Beginnings of the Honour of Clare', 119–41, for Richard of Tonbridge, and *VCH Surrey*, i. 280–1, for other Kentish feudal links.

other hand, consolidated Bletchingley and Chevington into one manor centred on Bletchingley Castle; here excavation has recently disclosed a massive 'double-pile' house of two storeys, dating from around the time of the Domesday survey and indicating a major baronial residence.[1]

Another great estate was formed so soon after the Domesday survey that it requires some reference here. In 1088 William de Warenne was created Earl of Surrey and endowed with extensive lands.[2] Despite his title the baronial *caput* was again outside the county, at Lewes in Sussex, but much of south-eastern Surrey (mainly land which had been Queen Edith's before the Conquest and royal demesne in 1086)[3] passed into his hands. To these manors, which included Reigate and Dorking, Warenne added Betchworth with its outliers in Leigh, Newdigate and Horley[4] to create a very substantial land-block centred on Reigate Castle, presumably built at this time. This re-grouping, which obscured some of the early land-divisions in Wealden Surrey, is analogous to the far more drastic restructuring of Sussex to create territories for the Warennes and other Norman lords.[5]

At a local level, the estate structure of Domesday Surrey combined ancient elements with relatively new ones.[6] One reason for this was the resilience of a small number of great institutional landlords, retarding the evolution of a land-market within the large tracts which they controlled; another was the contrasting economic and demographic development of the different zones of Surrey. The Crown, Chertsey Abbey and also the sees of Canterbury and Winchester still maintained, in more or less their original form, estates which had been formed centuries earlier. It may be equally significant, however, that the Chertsey ('Godley' Hundred) and Winchester (Farnham Hundred) estates lay largely on the infertile Bagshot Sand and Lower Greensand, which had some of the lowest densities of recorded population and plough-teams in 1086.[7] The other lightly settled area, the Weald, included manors such as Bramley, Dorking and Chevington which were broad swathes of territory several miles long. The densely farmed and settled area of north-east Surrey[8] had by contrast fragmented into numerous small, 'one-vill' manors, a gradual process of fragmentation which continued into the age of Domesday Book and after.

The royal vills, the great estate centres of mid-Saxon Surrey, now had direct economic control over only a residue of their former territories: but they were still considerably more important and complex than ordinary manorial demesnes. Their ancient role as administrative and tribute-collection-centres is only occasionally suggested in Domesday Book, as in the references to a villan at Kingston upon Thames 'for the purpose of collecting the Queen's wool', or to three tenants who 'could not withdraw without the king's precept because they were beadles at Kingston'.[9] Other indications are provided by place-names (for instance those of Norbiton and Surbiton, the north and south *beretuns*, or granges, of Kingston),[10] or by later sources such as the early fourteenth-century rental of Godalming royal manor which includes 'cotmen' responsible for hanging criminals.[11] Such details of local organization, which lay outside the Domesday commissioners' terms of reference, were none the less of great importance in the everyday life of the time.

By the end of the seventh century, kings had adopted the practice of endowing monasteries with so-called 'multiple estates': complexes of names and hidated land-units, containing numerous scattered farms and hamlets, which were alienated from their parent royal vills to be exploited from new estate centres.[12] Surrey examples recorded both in early charters and in Domesday Book are Chertsey (vills of Chertsey, Egham, Thorpe, Chobham, Woodham and *Huneuualdesham*), Farnham (vills of Farnham, Binton, Churt and elsewhere) and Battersea (vills of Battersea, 'Washingham' and Wandsworth).[13] Other large complexes still survived in 1086,

[1] Bird and Bird (eds.), *Archaeology of Surrey*, 253–4.
[2] See, for instance, Blair, 'Surrey Endowments of Lewes Priory'.
[3] Ibid. 110–12.
[4] Ibid. 104–9.
[5] For which, see J. F. A. Mason, 'The Rapes of Sussex and the Norman Conquest', *Sussex Archaeol. Collections* 102 (1964), 68–93.
[6] For what follows, see Blair, *Early Medieval Surrey*, Ch. 1.
[7] Darby and Campbell (eds.), *Domesday Geography*, 378–81.
[8] Ibid.
[9] GDB 30v, 32v.
[10] Gover *et al.* (eds.), *Place-Names of Surrey*, 63.
[11] Woods, 'Rental of the Principal Manor of Godalming'.
[12] For this interpretation, see Blair, 'Frithuwold's Kingdom'.
[13] Sawyer (ed.), S.1165, GDB 32v; S.382, GDB 31; S.1248, GDB 32. These are plotted in Blair, *Early Medieval Surrey*, fig. 9.

and although Domesday data are inadequate on their own for reconstructing multiple estates with their constituent vills, several can be interpreted in the light of later evidence; it can be shown, for instance, that Bramley (Æthelnoth TRE, Odo of Bayeux TRW) comprised the later townships of Shalford, Bramley, Wonersh, Hascombe and Dunsfold.[1]

But the great majority of manors in Domesday Surrey were of the small, self-contained kind that typically emerged as parishes during the next hundred years or so. Their development was intimately connected with the social and economic changes of the tenth and eleventh centuries, notably the formation of villages and of open field-systems. In regions of linear geology, manors tended to develop as strips running across the grain of the landscape to include several different soil-types within each unit. Thus on the dip-slope and scarp-slope of the Surrey Downs, where the different soils run in bands from west to east, the land-units fragmented into narrower and narrower strips running from north to south. A common clue to this process is the tendency for neighbouring pairs of manors to bear the same name, marking them as halves of an earlier whole: thus a sequence of parishes along the dip-slope are called (from west to east): West Clandon, East Clandon, West Horsley, East Horsley, Effingham, Little Bookham, Great Bookham. Domesday Book rarely records the 'surnames' of these split townships, and there is good reason to think that in 1086 they were often still at a formative and unsettled stage.[2]

The Church in Domesday Surrey had only experienced minor changes since the Conquest. Chertsey, the one great monastic house, retained its English abbot, Wulfweald; the Augustinian priories of Southwark and Merton, and the Cistercian Abbey of Waverley, had yet to be founded. The Cluniac Abbey of Bermondsey had only just been built, and Domesday Book describes it with uncharacteristic eloquence as 'a new and handsome (*pulchra*) church'.[3] For the ordinary people of Surrey the most important religious institutions were probably still the oldest, indeed the most old-fashioned: the Anglo-Saxon minsters.[4] Often founded during the first century of Anglo-Saxon Christianity, they were staffed by teams of priests ministering to the scattered inhabitants of large, multi-vill parishes. By 1086 the division of these parishes into smaller areas served by 'one-priest' churches was still far from complete, and most of the Surrey minsters are clearly visible in Domesday Book. Chertsey, Farnham, Woking and Bermondsey churches can be shown on charter evidence to have been founded for monastic communities in the late seventh and early eighth centuries; Godalming, Kingston upon Thames, Croydon, Southwark and Leatherhead were ancient and important churches by the Conquest, and may have been as old as the others. A particular ceremonial importance must have attached to Kingston, the coronation church of late Anglo-Saxon kings. Like minsters throughout England, most of them had come down in the world by 1086: impoverished, deprived of much of their old parochial authority, their revenues alienated to clerical absentees and pluralists. The foremost appropriator of Surrey minsters was one Osbern de Eu, who is listed as holding the churches at Farnham, Leatherhead and Woking;[5] Southwark Minster had fallen into Odo of Bayeux's clutches, and Godalming into Ranulph Flambard's.[6] The old minsters were fading away; yet their real demise came after 1100. In their status as parochial and cult centres, and in the local esteem which they enjoyed, it is probable that in 1086 they still outshone the little estate churches that were springing up so fast in the countryside.

Yet it was with the estate churches that the future lay.[7] It is impossible to know how many of those listed in 1086 had existed twenty years earlier. A handful of Surrey churches retain standing fabric which is stylistically or technologically Anglo-Saxon rather than Norman, but there is little reason to think that any of these pre-date the eleventh century,[8] and it is even possible that all were built after the Conquest. There are, however, certain patterns: for instance, manors held

[1] GDB 31; plotted in Blair, *Early Medieval Surrey*, fig. 9.

[2] F. W. Maitland, 'The Surnames of English Villages', *The Collected Papers of Frederic William Maitland*, ed. H. A. L. Fisher, ii (Cambridge, 1911), 84–95; Blair, *Early Medieval Surrey*, Ch. 1.

[3] GDB 30.

[4] For what follows, see Blair, *Early Medieval Surrey*, Ch. 4; J. Blair, 'Secular Minster Churches in Domesday Book', *Domesday Book: A Reassessment*, ed. P. H. Sawyer (London, 1985), 104–42; J. Blair, 'Parish Churches in the Eleventh Century', *Domesday Book Studies*, eds. Williams and Erskine, 65.

[5] GDB 31, 30v, 30.

[6] GDB 32, 30v.

[7] For what follows, see Blair, *Early Medieval Surrey*, Ch. 5; Blair, 'Parish Churches in the Eleventh Century', 65–8.

[8] The arguments to the contrary in Radford, 'Church of St Mary, Stoke D'Abernon', are not convincing.

by religious proprietors or by especially important laymen in 1066 seem abnormally well-endowed with churches in 1086. Architectural evidence suggests, predictably enough, that the larger post-Conquest Romanesque churches were built on demesne manors of the greater magnates, and also that small subinfeudated manors may have been acquiring churches especially rapidly around the time of Domesday Book and just after. It is at least clear that in Surrey as elsewhere the building of local churches was a process especially characteristic of the eleventh and early twelfth centuries, and well under way by 1066: the Norman settlement probably stimulated it, but did not cause a radical change of direction. The changes which eventually brought into being the modern parochial system were to come later, in the middle years of the twelfth century.[1]

The Domesday record of towns is notoriously incomplete, and Surrey is no exception: London, Southwark and Guildford are only mentioned incidentally, in the form of references to tenements or burgesses belonging to particular lords or particular rural manors. The king is said to have seventy-five tenements (*hagae*) in Guildford accommodating 175 men, and houses there also belonged to the nearby manors of Bramley and Shalford.[2] Tenements and burgesses in London (eighty attached to seven manors), in Southwark (thirty-five attached to eight manors), and 'in Southwark and London' (twenty-two attached to two manors)[3] belonged to estates widely scattered across the county, supporting Round's view that much of Surrey looked not towards Guildford but inevitably towards Southwark, which equally inevitably functioned as a suburb of London.[4] Soon afterwards, townsmen from Southwark and London can be observed investing in Surrey property: for instance, land at Addington held of the Archbishop by one Wulfsige of Croydon in the early 1090s had passed by *c.*1120 to Edward of Southwark and from him to the important Londoner Edward of Cornhill.[5]

London was always thereafter to exert an important influence on the development of Surrey, notably in the market which it offered for non-cereal goods such as timber, iron, bacon and fruit. These varied products were the more important in a county which lacked the natural resources to become a major grain-producer, and they mark Surrey as belonging more to the 'wood-pasture' than to the 'champion' zone of England. These characteristics must already have been apparent in the eleventh century, though as usual the Domesday data for non-arable resources are disappointing and presumably very incomplete.[6] Meadow, pasture and of course woodland were plentiful, though hard to quantify. Notable in the record of mills are the seven worth £42 at Battersea, a manor whose total value was only £75.[7] Byfleet, Petersham and an unnamed holding in Kingston Hundred produced renders of eels and lampreys;[8] a fishery at Kingston upon Thames was 'very good' (*valde bona*); while it is said of the Mortlake fishery that 'Harold set it up by force in King Edward's time in the land of Kingston and in the land of St Paul's'.[9] Chertsey had 'a forge which serves the hall', and Wandsworth a vine-dresser (though ostensibly no vineyard).[10] The two most unusual items are both in the entry for Limpsfield, which had three hawks' nests in the wood and two stone-quarries.[11]

Epilogue: Surrey 1066–1086

In assessing the long-term impact of the Conquest on English society, it is salutary to reflect on the conclusions that an archaeologist might draw if he had to interpret Anglo-Norman England without the benefit of written sources. Presumably he would notice the advent of new types of stone building, both military and religious, towards the end of the eleventh century, but he would be hard put to demonstrate that these were the consequences of an invasion. Looking ahead, however, he would find abundant physical evidence for growth, change and adaptation in

[1] For these themes, see papers in Blair (ed.), *Minsters and Parish Churches.*
[2] GDB 30, 35v.
[3] For details, see *VCH Surrey*, i. 286.
[4] Ibid. 275.
[5] F. R. H. Du Boulay, *The Lordship of Canterbury* (London, 1966), 339; PRO, DL27/46.
[6] For details, see Darby and Campbell (eds.), *Domesday Geography*, 390–405.
[7] GDB 32.
[8] GDB 34, 32v, 36.
[9] GDB 30v.
[10] GDB 32v.
[11] GDB 34.

many areas of life during the early to mid twelfth century: he might well be tempted to postulate that around 1130 England was invaded by members of some alien and more developed culture. The moral may be that although the Norman settlement was disruptive, destructive and savage, it assimilated more than it changed: the hidden strengths of Anglo-Saxon society survived to meet the opportunities and challenges of twelfth-century economic growth.

When we look at specifics, the Conquest seems damaging indeed. The drastic fall in the value of so many manors suggests that its immediate aftermath left Surrey badly scarred, though their recovery by 1086 is no less striking.[1] The inhabitants of north-western Surrey experienced only too well the new king's love of hunting, for their fields and farms were brought into his new Forest of Windsor.[2] The only direct Domesday reference to this is in the Pyrford entry, which states that 'the king has 3 hides of this land in his forest', though foresters are mentioned at Woking (TRE) and Walton-on Thames (TRW).[3] Stoke (in Guildford) is said to be 'in the king's park', presumably Guildford Park which later appears as one of the forest walks.[4] But most evident, of course, is the Norman policy of land-settlement: the expropriation of all the wealthiest Englishmen to make way for an alien ruling class.[5] Here, as so often, the effect was one of amalgamation: the greater baronies were often formed from the holdings of several pre-Conquest predecessors.[6] Charges of unjust or illegal expropriation, common in Domesday Book generally, are in Surrey levelled principally at Odo of Bayeux. At Southwark he usurped the king's dues and annexed the minster and waterway;[7] at Lambeth he stole a field from the church;[8] at Weybridge, Farncombe and Rodsall he seized land without authority;[9] while at Guildford his reeve of Bramley acquired one house by befriending its owner and another by marrying its heiress.[10] There are also specific cases in which the settlement can be seen to have disadvantaged the freer and more prosperous peasantry. The 'allodial tenants of the vill' who held ten hides in pre-Conquest Cuddington were gone by 1086, and at Wallington Richard fitzGilbert held a virgate 'whence he evicted a peasant who dwelt there'.[11]

Because such cases show that the stereotype of Norman oppression has substance, they also tempt us to forget that it is one-sided. Even on a surface view of the evidence, English thegns of middle and lesser rank often survived. The final section of the Surrey Domesday, 'the land of Osweald and other thegns', lists eight such (notably that hardy survivor Osweald, the Abbot of Chertsey's brother, who still held three of his old manors and had even acquired one of Harold's since 1066).[12] And a surface view would almost certainly be wrong, for it is likely that far larger numbers of small English proprietors remained in possession of their lands below the level of recorded tenure.[13] 'Wulfsige of Croydon', revealed by an exceptional source to be holding a knight's fee at Addington in the 1090s,[14] may stand for many of his unrecorded peers, probably the ancestors of more twelfth-century gentry families than we will ever know. Nor does the advent of Norman proprietors presuppose a radically different relationship between lord and land. Even if many of the new tenants-in-chief had much larger estates than their predecessors, they subinfeudated to mesne-tenants and knights who cleared wastes, built churches, and in other ways supervised the development of the landscape much as the late Anglo-Saxon thegns had done. If anything, the incentives created by assigning outlying portions of large manors to previously landless men are likely to have accelerated the processes of growth which were already in train.[15] In the long run even the restrictions imposed by forest law were more apparent than real, when population growth at last encouraged colonization of the Windsor Forest area during the twelfth and thirteenth centuries.[16]

Domesday Book is remarkable less for its record of conquest than for its record of Anglo-Saxon laws, customs and systems of organization respected and perpetuated in

[1] See p.5 above.
[2] For the forest, see *VCH Surrey*, i. 356–9.
[3] GDB 32, 30, 36.
[4] GDB 30.
[5] More fully discussed by Round, 'Introduction', *VCH Surrey*, i.
[6] See especially Mortimer, 'Honour of Clare', for the antecedents of Richard fitzGilbert's fief.
[7] GDB 32.
[8] GDB 34.
[9] GDB 31–31v, 32.
[10] GDB 30.
[11] GDB 31v, 30.
[12] GDB 36v.
[13] Cf. V. H. Galbraith, *The Making of Domesday Book* (Oxford, 1961), 153–5; P. H. Sawyer, '1066–1086: A Tenurial Revolution?', *Domesday Book: A Reassessment*, ed. Sawyer, 71–85.
[14] See p.15 above.
[15] As argued by Blair, *Early Medieval Surrey*, Ch. 2.
[16] Ibid.

Anglo-Norman society. Without the old English structure of shire and hundred it could never have been compiled; it is a monument to Norman energy, but also to a system more sophisticated than the Normans had ever known before. The very fact that it lists so many land-disputes, fought along English lines and settled in traditional English ways, speaks volumes for the basic stability of institutions. To study this great achievement of Norman government at a local level is to become ever more aware of ways in which the conquered society proved more resilient than that of the conquerors.

HUNDREDS AND WAPENTAKES

F. R. THORN

UNDER William I, as under the English kings, vills were grouped together for taxation, judicial and other obligations into 'hundreds' or, in former Danish areas, into 'wapentakes'. These administrative units, intermediate in size between the vill and the shire, and laid down before civil parishes came into existence, usually consisted of a single unified tract of territory (in 1086 varying widely between twenty and 300 hides in extent) which could belong to a variety of tenants-in-chief. Often a lord (particularly the king or a church) was paramount in a hundred; or the lordship of the hundred was attached to a particular manor by a system that was developed in the later medieval period. Some hundreds contained a single large manor only, and these and others had but a single tenant-in-chief. A few had isolated detachments and fewer still were ecclesiastical hundreds geographically scattered but owing suit to their church, however remote, and not to some local meeting-place. Vills were sometimes divided by hundred boundaries and the members of large manors were often in several different hundreds. Many of the hundred-names, if not replaced in 1086 by those of manors, refer to the meeting-places, 'moots', which were often at road-junctions, river-crossings, beside barrows or mounds, on hilltops or near isolated trees in a prominent position.

Hundreds cannot be described or mapped on the basis of Domesday Book alone, for the boundaries of estates and hundreds are never indicated, nor can every estate be allocated with certainty to a particular hundred, especially when it is mentioned in passing or is the dependency of some composite manor. The composition of hundreds can be partly restored from internal evidence by noting those places that fall directly beneath a hundred heading in the text and by identifying hundredal groupings which in many counties are inscribed in a standard sequence. However, the later history of the manor and of the hundred as well as geographical probability must also be employed and the hundredal rubrication itself examined, for it can be shown to be sometimes incorrect or deficient. The scribe's not infrequent errors are of only a few types and easily allowed for, and some restoration of missing headings can be made from the evidence of the text; but a decision sometimes has to be made to restore a hundred heading above a place from later evidence alone.

If these restorations are not made, Domesday will seem to allocate such a place to a different hundred, of which it will appear, owing to its geographical position, to be an improbable detachment. Allowance must be made for the fact that places lying close to the boundary of a hundred in 1086 may well be found in an adjacent hundred in the thirteenth-century surveys which are the first to show the composition of hundreds in detail.

Strictly speaking, it is impossible to map eleventh-century hundred boundaries. The hundred is the sum of exploited land and woodland, while 'waste', 'forest', moor and bog are either to be regarded as being outside the hundred, or the hundred boundary through them is ill-defined. Expansion of arable land, assarting, and drainage have all tended to change boundaries considerably. Compared with the number of vills surveyed in Domesday Book, charters with boundary clauses are few, their interpretation difficult and their relation to Domesday estates often indirect. Few estate maps survive from the Middle Ages and the first accurate hundred maps, dating from the early nineteenth century, are at the end of a process of change which may have left the 1086 pattern scarcely recognizable. But by using the evidence, whether certain, probable or supplemented, for the composition of the eleventh-century hundreds, lines can be drawn between manors—which may well contain more than one place and extend over more than one modern parish—according to the hundred in which they probably lay in 1086. In this way it is possible to recover something that approximates to eleventh-century topography and administrative divisions.[1]

THE HUNDREDS OF SURREY

Surrey was probably first defined in the ninth century, following its incorporation into Wessex, and at the same time attained roughly its recent extent.[2] In the

[1] Apart from works cited in individual articles in the series, documents and discussions concerning the hundredal system will be found in O. S. Anderson, *The English Hundred-Names* (Lund, 1934); *Inquisitions and Assessments Relating to Feudal Aids with other Analogous Documents, Preserved in the Public Records Office A.D. 1284–1431* (abbr. *Feudal Aids*), 6 vols. (HMSO, London, 1899–1920); F. Liebermann, *Die Gesetze der Angelsachsen*, 3 vols. (Halle, 1903–16); H. R. Loyn, *The Governance of Anglo-Saxon England, 500–1087* (London, 1984); A. J. Robertson (ed.), *The Laws of the Kings of England from Edmund to Henry I* (Cambridge, 1925); F. M. Stenton, *Anglo-Saxon England* (3rd edn., Oxford, 1971).

[2] This followed Egbert's victory in 825. At the time of the foundation of Chertsey Abbey 'the men of Surrey' formed a sub-kingdom of Mercia; see John Blair, 'An Introduction to the Surrey Domesday', p.7 above. A series of still-continuing boundary changes, beginning in 1889 with the creation of the Administrative County of London, much enlarged in 1965 into Greater London, has, of course, taken many of the northern parishes of Surrey into London.

Burghal Hidage, which appears to date from between 914 and 919,[1] its area is represented by 1,800 hides allotted to the *burh* of Southwark and by 600 hides to that of Eashing.[2] Surrey is not mentioned in the early eleventh-century County Hidage,[3] and it is not possible to give an exact total for the TRE hides supplied in Domesday Book, because it is never quite clear how many unnamed manorial subdivisions are duplicated by appearing as manors in their own right elsewhere.[4] Nevertheless, a sum of about 2,000 hides seems likely.[5] If the figure of the Burghal Hidage is not simply an ideal, representing the potential hidage of the county if heathland and the Wealden upland were brought under the plough,[6] then it is possible that the geld burden of the county, and so in effect its hidage (in so far as this was also a measure of geld liability), had already been reduced by 1066. By 1086 further remissions, unequally distributed, had reduced the total to about 700 hides.[7]

Domesday Book, however, does not speak of twenty-four or even twenty 'hundreds', but of thirteen, although in 1066 they ranged in size from 48¼ hides (Effingham Hundred) to 378 hides (Wallington Hundred).[8] To this number should almost certainly be added Farnham Hundred, co-extensive with the large manor of Farnham (sixty hides in 1066), an ancient possession of Winchester Church:[9] although hundredal rubrication is missing above the entry for the manor in Domesday Book, it was a hundred later in the Middle Ages and certainly a separate administrative unit from an early date.[10]

There was considerable dispute about tenure in Surrey when the Domesday survey was compiled; consequently there are a number of references to the work of the hundred courts.[11] One evokes the joint testimony of the 'men of the shire and of the hundred',[12] and one, emphatically, the 'men of the hundred, both French and English'.[13] But Domesday Book for Surrey, unlike the corresponding folios for Oxfordshire and Worcestershire which are more explicit, has little to say about the form, organization and interrelation of the hundreds themselves, although it goes out of its way to record a number of unnamed parts of holdings which did not lie in the same hundred as their parent manor.[14]

TABLE 1: The Hundreds of Surrey

Modern Name	Form(s) found in Domesday Book	Number on map
Blackheath	*Blacheatfeld, Blachedfeld, Blachefelde, Blachetfelle*	XI
Brixton	*Bricsistan, Brixiestan, Brixistan*	II
'Copthorne'	*Copededorne, Copedorne*	VIII
Effingham	*Fingeham*	VII
'Elmbridge'	*Amelebrige*	IV
*Farnham		IX
Godalming	*Godelminge*	X
'Godley'	*Godelei*	III
Kingston	*Chingeston, Chingestun*†	I
Reigate	*Cercefelle, Cherchefelle, Chirchefeld*	XIII
Tandridge	*Tenrige*	XIV
Wallington	*Waletone*	V
Woking	*Wochinges*	VI
Wotton	*Wodetone*	XII

* Does not occur as a hundred-name in Domesday Book.
† It is not absolutely certain how the abbreviated form *Chingest'* should be expanded.

Reconstruction of the hundreds that were the basis of the Domesday survey begins by using the Book's rubrication to isolate hundredal groups within the text; then the rubrication itself must be checked for completeness and accuracy against both internal and later evidence. Normally in Domesday Book all the manors belonging to one hundred are listed in each fief as a single block. Moreover, in many counties these hundredal blocks succeed one another in a standard sequence. These arrangements allow some groups of manors to be easily perceived and missing hundred heads restored, but neither principle applies to Surrey.[15] While a few individual hundreds tend to occur together in each chapter,[16] there is no fixed sequence and in several chapters the same hundred is entered more than once.[17] Nor does it seem that an alternative arrangement within the fief has been adopted, as is sometimes the case elsewhere in Domesday Book, by which the lands of each subtenant are grouped together. Yet there are signs in the form of displaced entries[18] and in the particular

[1] See D. Hill, 'The Burghal Hidage: the Establishment of a Text', *MA* 13 (1969), 84–92; S. Keynes and M. Lapidge (eds. and trans.), *Alfred the Great* (Harmondsworth, 1983), 193–4, 339–41; F. W. Maitland, *Domesday Book and Beyond* (Cambridge, 1897), 503.

[2] Eashing (in Godalming ancient parish) is at NGR SU 9443; its importance had probably been transferred to Godalming manor, or possibly to Guildford, by 1086. Variant versions of the Burghal Hidage allot 500, 600 and even 1,800 hides to Eashing.

[3] Maitland, *Domesday Book and Beyond*, 456.

[4] This perennial DB problem is discussed for Surrey in Baring, *Domesday Tables*, 14–16.

[5] Baring, *Domesday Tables*, 3. Maitland, *Domesday Book and Beyond*, 505, gives a total of 1,830 hides; on p.503 he erroneously gives 1,800 as the combined Burghal Hidage total for Southwark and Eashing.

[6] The same occurs in Wilts. where the Burghal Hidage total (4,800) considerably exceeds the DB total of *c.*4,000 hides.

[7] Baring, *Domesday Tables*, 3.

[8] These figures are from Baring, *Domesday Tables*, 17.

[9] See P. H. Sawyer (ed.), *Anglo-Saxon Charters: An Annotated List and Bibliography*, R. Hist. Soc. Guides and Handbooks, 8 (London, 1968) (henceforward cited by number preceded by S.), S.382, S.818, S.823; *VCH Surrey*, ii (1905), 579–81.

[10] See R. E. Glasscock (ed.), *The Lay Subsidy of 1334*, Brit. Acad. Records of Social and Economic Hist. ns 2 (London, 1975), 298; *Feudal Aids*, v (1908), 108.

[11] GDB 30, 30v, 31, 31v, 32(x4), 32v, 34(x2), 35(x2), 35v, 36(x3), 36v. In three cases (ff.31, 32v, 36v, concerning the manor of Mortlake, 2 hides in Tandridge Hundred, and the manor of Sutton (in Woking) respectively), those who 'say' or 'testify' are presumably the 'men of the hundred'.

[12] GDB 36.

[13] GDB 32.

[14] See Table 2, and discussion on p.20 below.

[15] Discussed in P. H. Sawyer, 'The "Original Returns" and Domesday Book', *EHR* 70 (1955), 177–97. He too recognizes no regular order in Surrey (p.181).

[16] A tendency for the material for the hundreds of 'Copthorne'/'Elmbridge'/Kingston and Brixton/Wallington/Tandridge/Reigate to be entered together (but not always in the same order) was noted by Baring, *Domesday Tables*, 1.

[17] See Chs. 5, 6, 8, 19, 36, and Morris (ed.), *Domesday Book: Surrey*, note to 5,13.

[18] On f.35v in the fief of Richard of Tonbridge, son of Count Gilbert, after the long entry for Thorncroft and before that for Effingham, seven lines of Latin comprising four entries have crept into the text from a return for 'Copthorne' Hundred: they have nothing to do with Richard's fief: see *VCH Surrey*, i (1902), 293.

TABLE 2: Manors in Surrey divided between Hundreds in 1086

Manor	Main holding	Subsidiary holding(s)
Bramley, f.31	In Blackheath Hundred, no. XI	2 hides probably in Woking Hundred, no. VI[1] 2½ hides in Wotton Hundred, no. XII[2]
Cuddington, f.31v	In 'Copthorne' Hundred, no. VIII	2 hides accounted for in Wallington Hundred, no. V
Gomshall, f.30v	In Blackheath Hundred, no. XI	1 hide in Wotton Hundred, no. XII
Merton, f.30	In Brixton Hundred, no. II	2 hides 'in another hundred'
Milton, f.36	In Wotton Hundred, no. XII	2 hides in 'Copthorne' Hundred, no. VIII[3]
Shere, f.30v	In Blackheath Hundred, no. XI	3 virgates in Wotton Hundred, no. XII

[1] The same two hides are recorded in a duplicate entry on f.34, where it is stated they were formerly a part of East Clandon in Woking Hundred. They are not said to lie in a different hundred in the entry on f.31.
[2] Stated to lie at Sutton (in Shere) in an apparent duplicate entry on f.32, but valued as part of Bramley.
[3] Apparently duplicated on f.35v, where an unnamed holding of two hides in 'Copthorne' Hundred, held by William fitzAnsculf, is stated to be valued 'in another hundred'.

nomenclature adopted for social groups,[1] that the material for Surrey had been arranged hundredally at one stage, as it had been in other counties.

On the other hand, the insertion of hundredal rubrication appears to have been carefully attended to. There are 107 actual headings and only occasional signs of inaccuracy: thus the word *Hund'* appears to have been omitted after 'Elmbridge' next to the unnamed one virgate held by Ealdgyth,[2] and the Wotton hundred heading above 'West Betchworth' (in Dorking)[3] probably belongs above the previous entry for Ockley.[4] About ten hundred-names are incorporated in the first sentence of the entry, and not placed, as normally, at the end of the first line or in a space at the end of the previous line.[5] Moreover, on folio 31v, by inserting an entry for one hide of land, held by Adam fitzHubert in Wallington Hundred (which was presumably intended as a parenthesis or as a part of the land of the previous manor), the scribe upset the sequence, for the places that follow (Cuddington, Ashtead, Tadworth, Fetcham, Mickleham and Great Burgh) are in fact in 'Copthorne' Hundred and governed by the hundred head above Pachesham. But in a similar context, in a list of lands dependent on Bramley on folio 31, the main scribe noticed that while Bramley itself and most of its dependencies were in Blackheath Hundred, two and a half hides of the manor (held by Ælfric TRE) were said to lie in Wotton Hundred. So, in order to make the sequence clear, he began a hundred head with *In* above the next entry but one, but left a gap; the correcting scribe completed this with *Blachefelde Hund'* which remained unrubricated. Occasional 'continuation' headings (*in ipso/hoc/eodem hundredo*, 'in this/the same hundred') also show a desire to remove ambiguity.[6] Nevertheless, it seems that about eight more hundred headings should be supplied; in most cases another part of the same vill is clearly rubricated in that particular hundred elsewhere in the text.[7] Failure to make such restorations leaves manors lying in hundreds from which they are geographically remote and to which they are not allocated by any later evidence.[8]

In the case of the Surrey hundreds, there is a comforting measure of agreement between those who have tried to restore the composition of the hundreds,[9] even though there continues to be uncertainty about the identification of a few settlements. Thus while one may follow John Morris in accepting *Mideham* and *Lodesorde* as scribal confusions for Mickleham and Lollesworth, and so not place *Lodesorde* in Sussex,[10] it seems less likely that *Orde* and *Brameselle* are respectively Worth and Branshill (both in Sussex): both are left unidentified in this edition.[11] As to the two occurrences of *Estreham*

[1] Baring, *Domesday Tables*, 9; Blair, 'Introduction', p.4 above.
[2] GDB 30v.
[3] GDB 35v; see p.21, n.2 below.
[4] Ockley appears immediately after Ockham which is said to lie in Woking Hundred. Although Ockham had land in Ockley in later times, there is no reason to think (*pace* Baring, *Domesday Tables*, 13–14) that Ockley was therefore a detached part of Woking Hundred. Such an arrangement has no certain parallel in DB for Surrey; moreover, Ockley was in Wotton Hundred in 1334 (Glasscock (ed.), *Lay Subsidy of 1334*, 299).
[5] For example, in two successive entries for 'Godley' Hundred (f.32v), one referring to Chertsey, the other to Thorpe.
[6] GDB 31, 32v, 35v(x2).
[7] Morris (ed.), *Domesday Book: Surrey*, supplies the following hundred heads, the name-forms in some cases differing from those used in this edition: Farnham above Farnham, f.31; Brixton above Southwark, f.32; Elmbridge above Weybridge, f.32v; Woking above Burpham, f.34v; Wotton above Ockley, f.35v (see n.4 above); Godalming above Witley, f.36; Brixton above Balham, f.36. It is doubtful whether Southwark as a borough requires a hundred heading, although there is a reference to the 'men of the hundred' within the entry. In addition, a Brixton hundred heading should be supplied above two occurrences of *Estreham* (ff.32v, 34), if indeed they are parts of Streatham (see p.21, n.1 below), and a 'Copthorne' hundred heading could helpfully be supplied above Cuddington on f.31v (see above).
[8] A literal following of the rubrication leads the *VCH* volumes into difficulties: for example, *VCH Surrey*, iii (1911), 246, puts the entry for Weybridge (f.32v) in 'Copthorne' Hundred, even though another portion (f.32) is squarely in 'Elmbridge'.
[9] The hundreds are considered or mapped in *VCH Surrey*, i, map between pp.294–5; *passim* in the *VCH Surrey* topographical volumes ii, iii, and iv (1912); in Baring, *Domesday Tables*, 1–37; in Morris (ed.), *Domesday Book: Surrey*; in Darby and Campbell (eds.), *Domesday Geography*, 364–5; and in O. S. Anderson, *The English Hundred-Names: The South-Eastern Counties* (abbr. *EHNSE*) (Lund, Leipzig, 1939), 57–66.
[10] Morris (ed.), *Domesday Book: Surrey*, notes to 19,41 and 36,9.
[11] *VCH Sussex*, vii (1940), 194, regards the Surrey *Orde* as Worth in Sussex, but the size of the church of Worth and the extent of the manor with its associated forests, as well as its subsequent history as a possession of the Warenne family and a member of the Rape and Barony of Lewes, suggest that the area of Worth does not correspond to *Orde*, but in 1086 was included by DB in its survey of Sussex, though unnamed. *VCH Surrey*, iii. 165, 217, is inclined to a 'Worth' in Reigate Hundred 'now commonly called "The Wor"', though it is not mentioned in Gover *et al.*, *Place-Names of Surrey* (abbr. *PNSurrey*); see Blair, 'Introduction', p.2 above. Morris's note on Branshill in *Domesday Book: Surrey*, note to 11,1, seems far-fetched.

identified by him as Ham in Richmond and Ham in Croydon, it is more probable that they are further parts of Streatham, even though hundredal rubrication would need to be restored in both cases.[1] Furthermore, as the text stands, *Becesworde* has to be 'West Betchworth' in Wotton Hundred, though it is possible that the larger Betchworth (formerly East Betchworth) in Reigate Hundred was in fact intended.[2]

Since there are very few cases where the evidence of Domesday Book and that of later documents conflicts,[3] it seems probable that there were few changes in the composition of the hundreds after 1086. But in restoring the extent of each hundred later evidence has to be used, for Domesday Book does not name all the places that lay in the county in 1086.[4] Although some hundreds can be confidently reconstructed because almost all the place-names that could conceivably belong to them are given by Domesday Book directly below a hundred head,[5] considerable tracts of land are still left without place-names. Thus, while hundred boundaries can mostly be drawn with confidence between nearby places which are allocated in Domesday Book to different hundreds, in areas of the county where named settlements are less dense it is only later documents that can indicate those members of manors or hundreds that Domesday Book tacitly engrosses in some other entry. However, one should not view late eleventh-century Surrey as a series of small settlements separated by unused heath and impenetrable forest: it is most improbable that there was still virgin land anywhere in the county (or in the adjacent Sussex and Kent), although the places named in Domesday Book tend to cluster in the central and north-eastern parts of the county.

Thus any mapping based on symbols of uniform size is misleading: whatever the nature of the land, in every county some manors or estates, treated by Domesday Book as single taxable units, were very large and, though given one name, must have contained several distinct named settlements at the time. Thus Farnham, assessed at sixty hides in 1066, no doubt comprised the area of the later parishes of Farnham, Seale, Elstead and Frensham and of the ten separate vills allotted to it in 1334.[6] In Woking Hundred the areas of the later parishes of Ash, Windlesham and Pirbright, unnamed in Domesday Book, were no doubt included in the statistics of some nearby large manor;[7] while the extents of the parishes of Bisley and Horsell were doubtless surveyed among the lands of the Abbot of Chertsey in 'Godley' Hundred. But in Surrey the absence of place-names is particularly related to the nature of one part of the county: in the southern densely wooded Wealden swathe the only named places are Witley and Hambledon in Godalming Hundred and Hartshurst and Ockley in Wotton Hundred, yet this need not imply an absence of exploitation or even of settlement. An impressive list can be compiled of parishes in this part of the county not mentioned and scarcely represented in Domesday Book: Alfold, Burstow, Capel, Charlwood, Chiddingfold, Cranleigh, Crowhurst, Dunsfold, Ewhurst, Godstone, Hascombe, Haslemere, Horley, Horne, Lingfield, Newdigate. The areas of such parishes are, however, to be sought either among the unnamed members of large nearby manors or—a local phenomenon—as the outliers of remoter settlements. The first explanation probably accounts for much of Godalming Hundred which would then have lain, unnamed and lumped together, in the twenty-four hides for which Godalming manor accounted in 1066. Likewise, Wonersh, Hascombe and Dunsfold probably lay in Bramley manor in Blackheath Hundred,[8] while the royal manors of Reigate and Dorking may well have had similar unnamed parts in Reigate and Wotton Hundreds respectively. Such manors had no doubt extended themselves up into the Weald as far as the boundary with Sussex, but their dependencies had yet to attain separate status and thus lay unnamed in the Surrey folios of Domesday Book.

The evidence from Kent and Sussex, whether from pre-Domesday place-names, from explicit statements in Domesday Book itself or from the additional material supplied by associated texts, is that many settlements in the Thames Basin or along the Sussex coast had outliers in the Weald.[9] Although the Surrey evidence is much less full, it is among the mentions of renders of timber, extents of woodland and in particular the pannage of pigs that Wealden outliers are to be suspected. The north-south alignment of the boundaries of all six southern hundreds (including the ecclesiastical franchise of Farnham) suggests corridors of land leading, like the rapes in Sussex and the lathes in Kent, from denser

[1] GDB 32v, 34. Neither Ham that he suggests is likely to have simplified from *Estreham*, which was already tentatively identified as Streatham by Baring, *Domesday Tables*, 1.

[2] If, as proposed above (p.20), the heading above *Becesworde* (f.35v) belongs with the previous entry, then a Reigate hundred heading could be inserted. In 1334 (Glasscock (ed.), *Lay Subsidy of 1334*, 299) East Betchworth (in Reigate Hundred, now simply Betchworth) was worth £5. 15*s.* 0¼*d.*, while 'West Betchworth' was worth £1. 13*s.* 7¼*d.* The author of *VCH Surrey*, iii. 166, erroneously thought that both Betchworth and 'West Betchworth' were separately mentioned in DB; in fact the same holding of 6 hides (TRE) is mentioned twice.

[3] See below p.24, n.3.

[4] In addition to *Feudal Aids*, v, and Glasscock (ed.), *Lay Subsidy of 1334*, the composition of the later medieval hundreds can be conveniently gleaned from *The Book of Fees*, 2 vols. and Index (HMSO, London, 1920–31), and the *Rotuli Hundredorum*, 2 vols. (Record Commission, London, 1812–18).

[5] For example, the 6 manors of Effingham Hundred all appear directly below hundred heads in DB; of the 18 vills in Brixton Hundred, only 5 have a manor that does not.

[6] Apart from Farnham itself, Glasscock (ed.), *Lay Subsidy of 1334*, 298, lists Wrecclesham, Frensham, Runwick, Churt, Elstead, Tilford, Runfold, Tongham, Badshot and Compton (near Farnham). This last is at NGR SU 8546, and is not the same as the Compton named in GDB 36.

[7] Ash was an unnamed part of Henley manor in Woking Hundred, f.34, held by Chertsey Abbey, whose hundred of 'Godley' was adjacent; see *VCH Surrey*, iii. 342.

[8] See Blair, 'Introduction', p.14 above.

[9] See the forthcoming 'Hundreds' articles for Kent and Sussex in this series. The important work on this topic for Surrey is by J. Blair, *Landholding, Church and Settlement in Early Medieval Surrey*, Surrey Archaeol. Soc. Research Vol. (forthcoming). References cited here are to J. Blair, 'Landholding, Church and Settlement in Surrey before 1300' (unpubl. D.Phil. thesis, Oxford Univ., 1982).

settlements at lower levels upwards to the Weald, facilitating transhumance and the exploitation of the woodland in other ways. Many of these Wealden areas will have originated a century or so before as pig-pastures; by the late eleventh century each probably had a name and contained a form of settlement, crude or temporary though it may have been. However, the only direct clue is afforded by the solitary reference to a woodland dene in the details of Ewell manor;[1] but pre- and post-Domesday evidence exists to reveal a network of outliers attached to manors which themselves lay in the northern hundreds of Surrey. Thus parts of Horley[2] were appurtenant to Sutton (near Cheam) and Banstead; Petridge Wood, Lake (Greatlake and Littlelake) and Thunderfield[3] to Merstham; Kingswood, Shellwood and Leigh[4] to Ewell; parts of Ockley to East Horsley and Ockham;[5] part of Burstow to Wimbledon.[6]

It is thus likely that the boundaries both of the hundreds and of the county had stabilized by 1086 and were very similar to those that survived into the nineteenth century.[7] So the boundaries on the map associated with this edition have been drawn between settlements as indicated by the text of Domesday Book; except where broken, these lines follow parish boundaries and the limits of hundreds as they appear on later maps, in the absence of any contradictory evidence from Domesday Book or other medieval texts.[8]

The resulting pattern is a simple one. With the exception of Farnham and 'Godley' Hundreds, which were ecclesiastical franchises, the first in the hands of Winchester Church, the second unequally divided between the churches of Chertsey and Westminster,[9] each of the hundreds of Surrey has a variety of tenants-in-chief: royal, ecclesiastical and lay. If Newdigate is discounted, for it was detached from 'Copthorne' Hundred in later times but not necessarily in 1086,[10] the only certain detachment seems to have been Windlesham, apparently isolated from Woking Hundred by the granting or confirmation of 'Godley' Hundred during the reign of Edward the Confessor.[11] The southernmost hundreds of Godalming, Blackheath, Wotton, Reigate and Tandridge share a similar shape and orientation, caused no doubt by their Wealden situation. The other hundreds are recognizably those of a southern English shire, and have in parts natural boundaries, some being delimited by the rivers Wey and Ember, others by the sharp edge of the escarpment that runs along the Downs from Guildford to Reigate. Yet only the hundreds of Kingston, 'Godley', Godalming and Reigate contain close on a hundred hides. Effingham at fifty hides is recognizably a half-hundred and was later named as such,[12] while 'Copthorne' with 197 hides is a double-hundred. But the figures for several hundreds are not close to a hundred hides or a multiple thereof, and it is not evident how a simpler pattern might be produced by notionally transferring hides from one hundred to another,[13] since those with excesses are not adjacent to those with deficiencies. Three of the most irregular—Brixton at $282\frac{3}{4}$ hides, Wallington at 378 and Tandridge at $210\frac{1}{4}$—form a vertical block bounded on the west by three of the most regular: Kingston at $101\frac{1}{2}$ hides, 'Copthorne' at 197 and Reigate at $106\frac{1}{2}$.[14] While a system based on eighty-hide units, as perhaps in Sussex, might explain the 495 hides (rightly 480 hides) that compose the western end of the

[1] GDB 30v: *unam denam silvae*. Swine-pasture in the Weald was granted in 727 as part of Cheam to Chertsey Minster (Sawyer (ed.), S.1181), but is not mentioned in DB.

[2] NGR TQ 2742. Horley was composed of a complex pattern formed by the outliers of other vills; see Blair, 'Landholding', 120.

[3] Petridge Wood, NGR TQ 276472; Greatlake and Littlelake, TQ 2944; Thunderfield, TQ 3042.

[4] Kingswood, NGR TQ 3542; Shellwood, TQ 2045; Leigh, TQ 2246.

[5] Both East Horsley and Ockham are listed in DB; on Ockham, see p.20, n.4 above.

[6] Burstow (on which see p.23, n.8 below) is at NGR TQ 3141; Wimbledon is at TQ 2470. The evidence for these dependencies is, for example, found or discussed in Sawyer (ed.), S.420/752, S.528, S.815; *VCH Surrey*, iii. 165; Baring, *Domesday Tables*, 13–14; Malden, 'Kingsland in Newdigate'; Blair, 'Introduction', pp.10–11 above.

[7] The older view of this question is well put by H. E. Malden (*VCH Surrey*, i, map between pp.294–5): 'The Hundreds to the south bordered on uninhabited forest, with no definite southern boundary, so that some isolated places in Sussex were reckoned as belonging to them'. Yet there is no certain evidence that any places that lay in Surrey or adjacent counties in 1086 were subsequently transferred by a change of boundary. For *Orde*, *Lodesorde* and *Brameselle*, see p.20 above.

[8] In the Wealden area of Surrey, where settlements named in DB are sparse or non-existent, the boundaries marked on the accompanying map follow those of later parishes but have been specially marked to show uncertainty. The boundaries of all the hundreds have been checked against A. Bryant, *Map of the County of Surrey, from an Actual Survey by A. Bryant in the years 1822 and 1823* (London, 1823), and C. and I. Greenwood, *Map of the County of Surrey from an Actual Survey made in the years 1822 and 1823* (London, 1823). Apart from the differences noted above (pp.20, 21) and a few variants of spelling, the identification of places and the composition of hundreds follow Morris (ed.), *Domesday Book: Surrey*. Baring's allocation to hundreds is similar, except some places are left unidentified and Ockley is put in Woking Hundred (see p.20, n.4 above).

[9] Westminster Abbey only held the manor of Pyrford (27 hides in 1066). For the charters relating to Farnham, see p.19, n.9 above; for the grant of 'Godley' Hundred, see n.11 below.

[10] If Newdigate was in 'Copthorne' Hundred in 1086, it would be a solitary exception to the rule that Wealden outliers are in Wealden hundreds, not in the hundreds of their parent manor. It is more likely, as is suggested in *VCH Surrey*, iii. 310, that in 1086 it lay in Wotton Hundred (where it has been mapped in this edition) as part of Dorking and that most of it was drawn into 'Copthorne' when it later became associated with the manor of Ashtead; but see Malden, 'Kingsland in Newdigate'.

[11] Sawyer (ed.), S.1094–5. It is specifically stated that the grant included the hundred of 'Godley'.

[12] For example, in Glasscock (ed.), *Lay Subsidy of 1334*, 301; see Anderson, *EHNSE*, 60. Effingham Hundred was sometimes in later ages treated as a unit with 'Copthorne' (*VCH Surrey*, iii. 320), out of which it might once have been carved.

[13] See Baring, *Domesday Tables*, 4, on the difficulties of rationalizing these figures. If an original hidage of 2,400 (see p.19 above) had been reduced by different amounts on different estates and in different hundreds (or reductions had taken place in some areas and 'new hides' been created in others), this could of course account for many or most of the differences in figures. For the comparable case of Cambs., see the forthcoming 'Hundreds' article in the present series.

[14] The hidage figures are those of Baring (*Domesday Tables*, 3, 17), adjusted by him by the elimination of suspected duplicates: Brixton, $282\frac{3}{4}$; Blackheath, 85; 'Copthorne', 197; Effingham, $48\frac{1}{4}$; 'Elmbridge', $122\frac{1}{4}$; Farnham, 60; Godalming, $97\frac{1}{2}$; 'Godley', 100; Kingston, $101\frac{1}{2}$; Reigate, $106\frac{1}{2}$; Tandridge, $210\frac{1}{4}$; Wallington, 378; Woking, $149\frac{1}{2}$; and Wotton, $59\frac{1}{4}$.

county, comprising the hundreds of 'Godley', Woking, Farnham, Godalming and Blackheath, such a scheme is not evident in the rest of the county.

A few details complicate the general picture. Firstly, while no vills appear to have been divided between hundreds, a number of manors—Bramley, Cuddington, Gomshall, Merton, Milton, and Shere—have parts that are said to be assessed in another hundred.[1] In those cases where this other hundred is named it is adjacent, and it is likely that the land of the manor simply spanned the boundary of the hundred, a pattern suspected, but rarely recorded, in other counties. Three entire holdings, however, are said to lie in one hundred but to be assessed in another: Great Burgh lay in 'Copthorne', but was valued in Wallington,[2] while two unnamed portions of 'Copthorne' Hundred—two hides held by the Abbot of Westminster and two hides held by William fitzAnsculf—were valued 'in another hundred'.[3] Secondly, as elsewhere in the kingdom, the county boundary is shown by Domesday Book to have cut through existing land-units, or perhaps ties of tenure had become more powerful than county administrations, so that land in one county had come to depend on that in another. In the case of Surrey one hide of Farnham lay in Hampshire;[4] Wallington had woodland in Kent;[5] and Merton had two sulungs, also in Kent, as a dependency.[6] Thirdly, one hide held by Earl Roger in Surrey belonged to his manor of Compton (near Chichester) in Sussex.[7] It is likely that Domesday Book is casual and sporadic in recording such linkages, and it is possible that there were more.[8] However, no Surrey vill had within it any manor or outlying portion of a manor that was part of another county.

As with the difficulty of rationalizing the hidage values of the various hundreds, so in other ways Domesday Book for Surrey affords little help in looking back to a more primitive stage of hundredal or county organization. It is hard to tie up Southwark and Eashing, the two centres named in the Burghal Hidage, with the royal vills named in King Alfred's will[9]—Eashing, Godalming, Guildford, Leatherhead, Thunderfield[10]—and in turn to relate these latter to the fourteen hundreds of Domesday Book. In some of the counties in Wessex, for example Hampshire, Somerset and Wiltshire, it is reasonable to suspect that at a stage earlier than Domesday Book the administration was concentrated on a series of royal vills, often distinguished by possessing minster churches.[11] This may well have been so, even at a stage before hidation and the laying out of shires. Thereafter, several hundreds of hides will often have depended on these royal *tunas*, but successive grants, sometimes of the *caput* itself, to laymen and churches may have led to the growth of smaller units of administration which evolved their own meeting-places. In other counties many such dominant manors are identifiable in Domesday Book as having been held by King Edward, often unhidated and responsible for a part or the whole of a day's or a night's farm. The closest examples of this type of royal manor in the Surrey folios are Woking, Stoke (in Guildford), Kingston upon Thames and Godalming, three of which are explicitly said never to have paid geld. Woking, Kingston upon Thames and Godalming gave their names to hundreds, and may, together with other similar, royal manors granted away by the Saxon kings, have been responsible for areas of territory larger than their 1086 hundreds, perhaps even for corridors of land—similar to the Sussex rapes—stretching from the Thames to the Weald.[12] 'Godley' Hundred, for example, had perhaps been granted out of land dependent on Woking. Even after the subdivision of these larger units, in some counties royal manors appear to have named and dominated some hundreds; in Surrey the hundreds of Reigate and Wallington are named from manors held by King William in 1086, but not formerly by King Edward.[13] Others however—Effingham, Tandridge and Wotton—though named from places recorded in Domesday Book, were not in royal hands either in 1066 or in 1086. Some of the other hundreds were named from places unnamed in Domesday Book but which lay in manors that themselves may once have dominated their hundreds: thus 'Godley' was a place in Chobham manor; Brixton lay

[1] The details are set out in Table 2, p.20 above. For Milton, see n.3 below.

[2] GDB 32.

[3] GDB 35v. But William fitzAnsculf's 2 hides appear to duplicate a part of his holding at Milton (f.36) which was in Wotton Hundred, where presumably the hides paid geld; see Table 2, p.20 above.

[4] GDB 31. It is not certain where this hide lay, although a further 10 hides (in 1066) lay at Bentley (NGR SU 7844) just inside Hampshire (f.40v). In later times at least, Bentley shared the same hundred court, at 'Blackheathfield' (in Farnham), with the bishop's Surrey land, but the manor may well have lain in a Hampshire hundred in 1086; see Thorn, 'Hundreds and Wapentakes', *Hampshire Domesday*, 31, n.7.

[5] GDB 30.

[6] GDB 30. It is possible that a corridor of land on the eastern edge of Surrey including Croydon (once a possession of the Church of Canterbury) had previously been in Kent, because Wallington, Titsey, Limpsfield and Lingfield all had outliers in Kent; see J. E. A. Jolliffe, *Pre-Feudal England: the Jutes* (Oxford, 1933), 91, and Blair, 'Landholding', 43.

[7] GDB 34. Not mentioned in the corresponding Sussex entry (f.24).

[8] But J. Morris (ed.), *Domesday Book: Sussex* (Chichester, 1976), note to 2,9, is incorrect in stating that Burstow (NGR TQ 3141) was evidently an outlier of West Tarring (Sussex, TQ 1304) according to the Domesday Monachorum (D. C. Douglas (ed.), *The Domesday Monachorum of Christ Church, Canterbury* (London, 1944), 99). *Buresto* (which is not certainly identified as Burstow) is there listed independently between *Terringes* (West Tarring) and *Pagaham* (Pagham, Sussex).

[9] Sawyer (ed.), S.1507.

[10] For Eashing and Thunderfield, see p.19, n.2 and p.22, n.3 above; the other places are mentioned in DB.

[11] Discussed in P. H. Hase, 'The Development of the Parish in Hampshire, particularly in the Eleventh and Twelfth Century' (unpubl. Ph.D. dissertation, Cambridge Univ., 1975); see also Stenton, *Anglo-Saxon England*, 299–302, and the relevant 'Hundreds' articles in the present series

[12] Leatherhead, mentioned in Alfred's will (n.9 above), had clearly once been an important manor, but in DB only its church is mentioned, by then attached to the manor of Ewell (f.30v). Presumably the manor had been broken up and its remaining parts, which cannot readily be identified, were in others' hands in DB. On the whole question of royal manors and minster churches, see Blair, 'Landholding', 35–40.

[13] Reigate had been held by Queen Edith; for Wallington no TRE holder is given.

in Lambeth; Blackheath lay in Wonersh, probably an unnamed member of Bramley manor. Other hundreds may have been dominated by an important manor, though not named from it: perhaps 'Copthorne' was by Ewell, which was itself possibly the rump of the former royal centre of Leatherhead. Brixton Hundred may have been presided over by Bermondsey or Merton, both held by Harold TRE, Blackheath Hundred by Gomshall, also held by Harold, and Wotton Hundred by Dorking, once held by Queen Edith.[1] But the comparative insignificance of some moot sites and of the manors that contained them may be a sign that their hundreds had once been part of larger units dominated by more important manors, or that the hundred-system had once been mainly independent of the lordship of manors. There is, however, no clear pattern, nor any sign that, apart from the ecclesiastical hundreds of 'Godley' and Farnham, any hundred was subject in 1086 to an individual's authority.[2] Moreover, the evidence provided by the Surrey folios does not enable a clear answer to be given to the question as to whether multiples of hundreds of hides had once depended on a few royal centres which had progressively lost their influence, or whether individual hundreds, long separate and devolved, were increasingly being dominated by a major manor and sometimes had recently been named from it.

Whatever changes produced the 1086 pattern, however, they were of lasting effect: with a few minor alterations involving individual manors, both the names and the extents of the late eleventh-century hundreds continued through the Middle Ages until the nineteenth century.[3]

[1] See Table 3 opposite.

[2] By 1316 (*Feudal Aids*, v. 106–11) the 'lordship of the hundred' was in individual hands: Farnham and 'Godley' Hundreds were still in the hands of their 1086 church holders. Godalming Hundred was held by the Bishop of Salisbury, 'Elmbridge' by Roger of London, Kingston by the queen, and Brixton, Tandridge, Woking, Blackheath, Wotton, Reigate and Wallington by the king. How far this notion of ownership stretched back in time and how far the hundred was attached to a particular manor is controversial; see H. M. Cam, *Liberties and Communities in Medieval England: Collected Studies in Local Administration and Topography* (Cambridge, 1944; repr. London, 1963), 64–90.

[3] See Table 3. The contents of each hundred seem to have been virtually the same in the fourteenth as in the eleventh century. By 1334, however, Limpsfield had become a liberty of the Abbot of Battle (Glasscock (ed.), *Lay Subsidy of 1334*, 303). There were a few subsequent changes, such as the transfer of Chessington to 'Copthorne' Hundred by the seventeenth century (*VCH Surrey*, iii. 481).

TABLE 3: The Domesday hundreds of Surrey, showing the places from which they were named, and their approximate relationship to the fourteenth-century hundreds

Modern Name and Number on map	Place from which named, with NGR if known and if not indexed below	Approximate relationship to the hundreds of the fourteenth century[1]
Blackheath, XI	Blackheath in Wonersh parish (TQ 0346)	Continued as Blackheath
Brixton, II	Brixton in Lambeth (TQ 3175); possibly an unnamed part of the Domesday manor of Lambeth	Continued as Brixton
'Copthorne', VIII	Name lost; site uncertain, but possibly part of the Domesday manor of Ashtead[2]	Continued as 'Copthorne'
Effingham, VII	Domesday manor (Abbey of Chertsey/ Richard of Tonbridge, son of Count Gilbert)[3]	Continued as the (half-)hundred of Effingham
'Elmbridge', IV	Formerly the name of a bridge on the old London-Chertsey road[4] over the river 'Emele' (now the Ember or Mole)	Continued as 'Elmbridge'
Farnham, IX	Domesday manor (Bishop of Winchester). The moot was in 'Blackheathfield' at Lawday House[5]	Continued as Farnham
Godalming, X	Domesday manor (royal)	Continued as Godalming
'Godley', III	Name lost; site uncertain, but probably in Chobham parish[6]	Continued as 'Godley'
Kingston, I	Domesday manor of Kingston upon Thames (royal)	Continued as Kingston
Reigate, XIII	Domesday manor (royal); formerly called 'Crutchfield' (DB *Cherchefelle*)[7]	Continued as Reigate
Tandridge, XIV	Domesday manor (Richard of Tonbridge, son of Count Gilbert)[8]	Continued as Tandridge
Wallington, V	Domesday manor (royal)	Continued as Wallington
Woking, VI	Domesday manor (the king/Bishop of Exeter)[9]	Continued as Woking
Wotton, XII	Domesday manor (Osweald)	Continued as Wotton

[1] Information is derived from Glasscock (ed.), *Lay Subsidy of 1334*, 297–303, and *Feudal Aids*, v. 106–11.

[2] Held by the Bishop of Bayeux. 'Copthorne' survived as a field-name in Ashtead parish until the mid nineteenth century; Gover *et al.*, *PNSurrey*, 67–8.

[3] The site of the moot is uncertain, but in the time of Edward I the sheriff's tourn was at a lost 'Lethe Croyce' and the joint leet of Effingham and 'Copthorne' Hundreds at a lost 'Leithepitt'; *VCH Surrey*, iii. 320.

[4] The bridge presumably lay to the west of Esher at TQ 1264, where the river Mole (formerly the 'Emele') defines the boundary of the parishes of Esher and Walton-on-Thames; see *VCH Surrey*, iii. 441; Gover *et al.*, *PNSurrey*, 86; Anderson, *EHNSE*, 60.

[5] 'Blackheathfield' is now represented by Heath End (SU 8549) and Heath House (SU 8149); Lawday House Farm is at SU 8249. See Anderson, *EHNSE*, 62; Gover *et al.*, *PNSurrey*, 165; *VCH Surrey*, ii. 579–80.

[6] Held by Chertsey Abbey. Last represented in the mid nineteenth century by the field-name 'Godley Hall Field' in Chobham parish (SU 9761). The hundred court was held at Hardwick, now represented by Hardwick Cottages and Hardwick Court Farm (TQ 027655) in Chertsey parish; *VCH Surrey*, iii. 396–7; Gover *et al.*, *PNSurrey*, 103; Anderson, *EHNSE*, 61.

[7] See Anderson, *EHNSE*, 64; Gover *et al.*, *PNSurrey*, 282, 304; *VCH Surrey*, iii. 165–6. On the replacement in the late twelfth century of the name 'Crutchfield' by Reigate (which affected both the manor and the hundred-name), see *VCH Surrey*, iii. 229, 234.

[8] The moot was half a mile north-west of Tandridge at the junction of the A25 with a minor road running north to Woldingham (TQ 369519); Anderson, *EHNSE*, 66; *VCH Surrey*, iv. 251; Gover *et al.*, *PNSurrey*, 308.

[9] The moot was at 'Harmes Hatch' in Send-with-Ripley parish, near the boundary with Ockham and Cobham parishes; Gover *et al.*, *PNSurrey*, 135; Anderson, *EHNSE*, 61; *VCH Surrey*, iii. 339.

BIBLIOGRAPHY

INDICES

TO THE DOMESDAY FOLIOS

BIBLIOGRAPHY

The following bibliography, arranged in date order, is derived by kind permission from D. Bates, *A Bibliography of Domesday Book*, published by Boydell and Brewer Ltd for the Royal Historical Society, 1986. Dr Bates has added certain entries to this county list in order to update it, and to include appropriate references which are cited in the 'General Studies' section of his original work.

SURREY

1. S. Henshall and J. Wilkinson, *Domesday; or an Actual Survey of South-Britain* (London, 1799). A translation of Surrey DB with no attempt to identify the place-names.

2. O. Manning and W. Bray, *The History and Antiquities of the County of Surrey*, 3 vols. (London, 1804–14). Vol. i contains a facsimile of the Surrey DB folios and an extended Latin text.

3. A. Hussey, *Notes on the Churches of Kent, Sussex and Surrey Mentioned in Domesday Book and Those of More Recent Date including Comparative Lists of the Churches and Some Account of the Sepulchral Memorials and Other Antiquities* (London, 1852).

4. H. James (director), *Domesday Book: or the Great Survey of England of William the Conqueror, A.D. MLXXXVI. Facsimile of the Part Relating to Surrey*. Photozincographed by Her Majesty's Command at the Ordnance Survey Office, Southampton (Southampton, 1861).

5. Anon., *A Literal Extension of the Latin Text, and an English Translation, of Domesday Book in Relation to the County of Surrey* (London, 1862).

6. H. E. Malden, 'The Domesday Survey of Surrey', *Domesday Studies: being the Papers Read at the Meetings of the Domesday Commemoration 1886*, ed. P. E. Dove, 2 vols. (London, 1888–91), ii. 459–70.

7. F. H. Baring, 'The Conqueror's Footprints in Domesday', *EHR* 13 (1898), 17–25. Reprinted with 'some additions and alterations' in F. H. Baring, *Domesday Tables*, see 15 below, 207–16. See also 29, 30.

8. F. H. Baring, 'The Hidation of Some Southern Counties', *EHR* 14 (1899), 290–9.

9. J. H. Round, 'Ingelric the Priest and Albert of Lotharingia', *The Commune of London and Other Studies* (London, 1899), 28–38.

10. H. E. Malden, 'Blechingley Castle and the De Clares', *Surrey Archaeol. Collections* 15 (1900), 17–26. For the Surrey DB estates of the Clares. See 35.

11. J. H. Round, 'Introduction to the Surrey Domesday', *VCH Surrey*, ed. H. E. Malden, i (London, 1902), 275–93.

12. H. E. Malden, 'The Text of the Surrey Domesday', ibid. 295–328.

13. H. E. Malden, 'Thunderfield Castle', *Surrey Archaeol. Collections* 18 (1903), 1–8. Suggests an identification for an unnamed Chertsey Abbey estate, cf. 12, 32.

14. H. E. Malden, 'Villeinage in the Weald of Surrey', *Surrey Archaeol. Collections* 20 (1907), 143–52.

15. F. H. Baring, *Domesday Tables for the Counties of Surrey, Berkshire, Middlesex, Hertford, Buckingham and Bedford and the New Forest* (London, 1909).

16. F. H. Baring, 'The Making of the New Forest', *EHR* 27 (1912), 513–15. A note argues that DB values suggest that in 1066 William's army may have crossed the Thames at Hampton.

17. A. Bonner, 'A Note on the Name "Battersea"', *Trans. of the London and Middlesex Archaeol. Soc.* ns 2 (1913), 434–7.

18. A. Bonner, 'Surrey Place-Names', *Surrey Archaeol. Collections* 36 (1925), 8?–101. Limited in content.

19. H. E. Malden, 'The Historical Geography of the Wealden Iron Industry', ibid. 107–10. For DB settlement in the Weald.

20. W. Farrer, 'The Honour of Wallingford', *The Boarstall Cartulary*, ed. H. E. Salter (Oxford, 1930). For the holdings of Robert d'Oilly and Miles Crispin.

21. H. E. Malden, 'Kingsland in Newdigate and Newdigate in Copthorne Hundred', *Surrey Archaeol. Collections* 39 (1931), 147–9. Identifies an unnamed settlement in Brixton Hundred, cf. 32.

22. E. H. Kennedy, 'The Domesday Mill at Bletchworth', *Surrey Archaeol. Collections* 40 (1932), 120–2.

23. J. E. B. Gover, A. Mawer and F. M. Stenton (in collaboration with A. Bonner), *The Place-Names of Surrey*, EPNS 11 (Cambridge, 1934).

24. B. W. Kissan, 'Lanfranc's Alleged Division of Lands between Archbishop and Community', *EHR* 54 (1939), 285–93. For the DB account of Canterbury's lands in nine counties.

25. A. T. Ruby, 'The Manor of Pachenesham, Leatherhead', *Surrey Archaeol. Collections* 55 (1958), 7–17.

26. E. M. Yates, 'A Study of Settlement Patterns', *Field Studies*, 1, no. 3 (1961), 65–84. For the Reigate, Dorking and Guildford areas.

27. H. C. Darby and E. M. J. Campbell (eds.), *The Domesday Geography of South-East England* (Cambridge, 1962).

28. D. Nail, 'The Meeting Place of Copthorne Hundred', *Surrey Archaeol. Collections* 62 (1965), 44–53.

29. D. Butler, *1066: the Story of a Year* (London, 1966). See 7, 30.

30. C. H. Lemmon, 'The Campaign of 1066', *The Norman Conquest: its Setting and Impact*, eds. D. Whitelock *et al.* (London, 1966), 77–122. See 7, 29.

31. W. E. Wightman, *The Lacy Family in England and Normandy, 1066–1194* (Oxford, 1966).

32. J. Morris (ed., from a draft translation by S. Wood), *Domesday Book: Surrey* (Chichester, 1975). For additions and corrections, see J. Morris (ed.), *Domesday Book: Hertfordshire* (Chichester, 1976); J. Morris (ed.), *Domesday Book: Bedfordshire* (Chichester, 1977).

33. B. Harvey, *Westminster Abbey and its Estates in the Middle Ages* (Oxford, 1977).

34. J. Blair, 'The Surrey Endowments of Lewes Priory before 1200', *Surrey Archaeol. Collections* 72 (1980), 97–126.

35. R. Mortimer, 'The Beginnings of the Honour of Clare', *Proc. of the Battle Conference 1980*, iii (1981), 119–41, 220–1.

36. J. Blair, 'The Early History of Horne: an Addendum', *Surrey Archaeol. Collections* 73 (1982), 179–80. For the DB manor of Chevington.

SURREY

37. M. Alexander, 'The Mills of Guildford', *Surrey Archaeol. Collections* 74 (1983), 91–9.

38. D. J. Gerhold, 'In Defence of Anglo-Saxon Putney and Roehampton', *The Wandsworth Historian*, 36 (1983), 6–16.

39. J. C. Ward, 'The Place of the Honour in Twelfth-Century Society: the Honour of Clare 1066–1217', *Proc. of the Suffolk Inst. of Archaeol. and Nat. Hist.* 35 (1983), 191–202.

The following volumes are those of the Alecto County Edition of Domesday Book which have been published to date. Included for convenience are the names of the authors who have contributed the 'Introductions' to each volume. All the articles on 'Hundreds and Wapentakes' have been written by F. R. Thorn.

1. A. Williams and R. W. H. Erskine (eds.), *The Northamptonshire and Rutland Domesday* (London, 1987).

   D. N. Hall, 'An Introduction to the Northamptonshire Domesday', ibid.

   T. D. Cain, 'An Introduction to the Rutland Domesday', ibid.

2. A. Williams and R. W. H. Erskine (eds.), *The Berkshire Domesday* (London, 1988).

   N. A. Hooper, 'An Introduction to the Berkshire Domesday', ibid.

3. A. Williams and R. W. H. Erskine (eds.), *The Buckinghamshire Domesday* (London, 1988).

   J. Bradbury, 'An Introduction to the Buckinghamshire Domesday', ibid.

4. A. Williams and R. W. H. Erskine (eds.), *The Cornwall Domesday* (London, 1988).

   I. N. Soulsby, 'An Introduction to the Cornwall Domesday', ibid.

5. A. Williams and R. W. H. Erskine (eds.), *The Herefordshire Domesday* (London, 1988).

   C. P. Lewis, 'An Introduction to the Herefordshire Domesday', ibid.

6. A. Williams and R. W. H. Erskine (eds.), *The Worcestershire Domesday* (London, 1988).

   A. Williams, 'An Introduction to the Worcestershire Domesday', ibid.

7. A. Williams and R. W. H. Erskine (eds.), *The Gloucestershire Domesday* (London, 1989).

   A. Williams, 'An Introduction to the Gloucestershire Domesday', ibid.

8. A. Williams and R. W. H. Erskine (eds.), *The Hampshire Domesday* (London, 1989).

   B. J. Golding, 'An Introduction to the Hampshire Domesday', ibid.

9. A. Williams and R. W. H. Erskine (eds.), *The Somerset Domesday* (London, 1989).

   G. A. Loud, 'An Introduction to the Somerset Domesday', ibid.

10. A. Williams and R. W. H. Erskine (eds.), *The Wiltshire Domesday* (London, 1989).

   N. A. Hooper, 'An Introduction to the Wiltshire Domesday', ibid.

INDEX OF PLACES

NOTES

In this edition, the place-names found in the translation, on the county map, and in the following Index of Places are all interrelated and have been established according to strict editorial policy. The central source for each of these three elements has been a specially compiled card-index containing a card for every mention of a place-name in Domesday Book: this index itself has been adjusted as research progressed. Thus the separate disciplines of identification, map-making, indexing, and rendering the Latin into readable English have all contributed to this compendium of Domesday place-names and to the manner of the presentation of each category. However, a word of caution is appropriate here, because the reader should be aware that the simple exchange of a Domesday name for even the most obvious modern equivalent does not necessarily mean that the original settlement lay precisely at that location, nor that it had a similar territorial form.

It is important to realize that the place-names of Domesday Book do not represent modern religious, social, administrative or agricultural units such as parishes, townships, villages, hamlets or farms, except by coincidence. They stand for estates or taxable units that may not in reality have been either independent or self-supporting. No bounds are given and these estates, depending on their size, may well have extended over more than one modern parish, be interlaced with other holdings, or possess a number of widely scattered members. Most Domesday estates will have contained several settlements, all of which had names in 1086, but which the survey leaves unnamed and whose statistics it engrosses with others. Frustratingly, Domesday says nothing that allows us to determine the centre, the extent, or the form of the estate.

Many Domesday estate-names will doubtless have been those actually current in the locality concerned; but others are 'book-names'—administrators' designations and often very general in scope—such as the name of a valley, hill, river or tract of land. These were probably known by more specific names on the ground, but Domesday Book does not record them. Especially where a vill is shown to have been in divided ownership in 1086, or where the Domesday unit is the fragment of some great multiple estate of pre-Conquest times, Domesday may well retain the 'charter' or 'book' name of its more extensive predecessor even though other evidence may indicate that a more precise appellation was almost certainly in use at the time.

The Domesday name may now be represented by a parish name, or by that of a township, hamlet or isolated farm. It may no longer survive as a settlement-name at all, but only as that of a river, wood, hill, road or bridge. The name may even have become lost before it appeared on any map; and finally it may have escaped identification altogether, either because the place designated scarcely survived the eleventh century or because the form in which Domesday transmits the place-name is corrupt and so far unintelligible.

A Domesday place can only be considered to be satisfactorily identified when the proposed name has passed a number of tests. Is the evolution of the 1086 name-form to the suggested modern equivalent philologically acceptable? Does it lie in the hundred indicated or implied by the text, or reconstructed from it? Do the details of land, equipment, resources and industry given by the entry in Domesday Book accord with what could have been practicable within the proposed area? Can the estate be identified among the possessions of the 1086 holder's heir or successors in later centuries? In practice, by no means all published identifications satisfy these requirements and the accuracy and reliability of identifications varies considerably from county to county. Much depends on the quality of the work of the eighteenth and nineteenth century 'antiquarian' pioneers and of the sections on Domesday in the relevant volume of the *Victoria County Histories*. The standard of more recent work, the existence of a county volume among the publications of the English Place-Name Society, or of 'topographical' volumes from the *Victoria County History* make the identifications of some counties more secure than those of others. The evidence so gathered will have been reviewed for H.C. Darby's monumental series on Domesday Geography (1952–77) and for the Phillimore edition of Domesday Book (1975–86), but with varying thoroughness. For the present publication, it has been impractical to re-examine every item of this complex and widely scattered evidence afresh, but in cases where modern published identifications conflict or where there are other obvious reasons for doubt, the evidence has been rescrutinized.

In the following Index of Places, a system of square-bracketed editorial additions and of single or double inverted commas imply varying degrees of certainty in identification, and are set out in the key below. A further key precedes the translation in this volume and contains the related conventions employed there. Among the symbols on the county map, of which this index is also the gazetteer, will be found a system of circles, complete, broken or interlinked, which serves the same function, besides a full treatment of the county and hundred-boundaries in 1086.

By far the greater part of the evidence for the identification of place-names is derived from Great Domesday Book itself. However, occasionally a holding was entered without its eleventh-century name, or the name given has been replaced by a later one, and where possible these have been supplied from the testimony of certain other documents that are directly related to the making of Domesday Book or to its use. Such documents deemed admissible as evidence in this context are, for example, the Exon Book for the south-western counties, Evesham A for Worcestershire, and the Herefordshire Domesday. However, there is no source other than the Domesday folios accepted for identifications in this volume.

F.R.Thorn

GENERAL

1. Scope of Index

The Index refers to all place-names found in the text written at the time of the compilation of Great Domesday Book, 1086–7, including all contemporary corrections, notes and additions in the margins. Insertions added to the MS in medieval and later times are not indexed, but identifications are incorporated which have been assisted by the evidence of any secondary documents that might exist as indicated in the introduction to these notes above.

Only references to the folios and translation supplied with this volume are indexed. A section listing any named holdings in this county which are recorded in the folios of other shires will be found on the associated county map.

2. Use of suprascript numbers

Where a place-name occurs more than once on a folio, its incidence is indicated by a suprascript number.

Note that occasionally a named entry can be followed immediately by further reference(s) to the same vill, usually designated by terms such as *ibi*, 'there'; *ibidem*, 'in the same place'; *in eadem villa*, 'in the same vill'. Such entries are not indexed as the place-name itself is absent.

3. Use of "...."

Double inverted commas indicate a name found only in Domesday Book and for which there is no known later equivalent, or of which the form may be corrupt. The name so enclosed is printed in Roman type.

4. Use of '....'

Single inverted commas indicate the latest or most typical known form of a name which remained in use beyond the eleventh century, but which either has not survived into modern times at all, or which only appears on twentieth-century maps as the name of a feature such as a river, hill, wood etc., rather than a place of habitation. This also applies to names without a continuous history and which have only recently been revived for antiquarian reasons.

MODERN PLACE-NAMES (ROMAN TYPE)

5. Authority

The modern place-names are consistent with those marked on the particular 1:100,000 Ordnance Survey grey base-map employed as the background for each associated county map. Note that place-names can vary from edition to edition of OS maps and their absence from this particular map does not mean they are necessarily lost.

6. Modern counties

Throughout this edition the county-boundaries are regarded as those that existed prior to the restructuring of the counties in 1974.

7. National Grid Reference

Four-figure National Grid References are given for modern place-names which represent settlements recorded in Domesday Book. Note that these NGRs do not necessarily pin-point the precise location of such settlements in 1086 for the reasons set out in the introduction to these notes above.

8. Common prefixes and suffixes: Great, Little, etc.

Modern places which are distinguished by common prefixes such as Old, Great and Little, Upper, Middle and Lower, Nether and Over, East and West, North and South have their main entry indexed under the relevant place-names, in the same way as those with distinguishing suffixes such as All Saints, St Andrews and Abbots.

9. Use of 'or', 'and'

Where a place is designated by two or more prefixes or suffixes and linked by 'or', e.g. Great or Little, All Saints or St Andrew, it is uncertain which of these two modern places represents the holding in question or whether both did so. Where prefixes are linked by 'and', e.g. East and West, St Peter and St Martin, the inference is that both modern places lie within the territory of a single estate of 1086.

10. Use of 'in', 'near'

In the event of two or more places in one county having the same name, they are distinguished by the addition of the parish-names in square brackets, e.g. [in Compton]. The only exception is when the parish- and place-name are the same, or where the place-name forms part of the parish-name. In these cases one will be followed by the parish-name, [in Compton], while the other will be related to a prominent nearby town or feature, [near Wallingford].

11. Choice of representative names distinguished by affixes

In a given locality a single place-name in Domesday Book may now be represented by a number of variant names distinguished by different prefixes or suffixes. Where a major derivative name signifying a village or hamlet still exists, such as Great, Little, Higher, Lower, St Mary, St Peter, this is preferred to minor or dependent variant names, such as Park, Moor, Gate, Green, Manor. Similarly minor settlement-names, where only they survive, are preferred to non-settlement names such as those of fields, hills, woods, streams, marshes.

Where the name in Domesday Book is represented on modern maps only by the name of a minor feature, the principal element alone is used in the index and in the translation, so that Weston Farm, Lodge, Hall, Bridge, Wood etc., appear only as Weston.

12. Places now 'lost'

A number of places named in Domesday Book either no longer exist as distinct settlements or have disappeared altogether due to urban development, inundation by reservoirs, coastal erosion, rural depopulation, and other causes. These 'lost' places are treated variously, both in the translation and in this index, according to the circumstances that have caused them to disappear.

a. Places which have been absorbed into an area of urban development, but have given their name to a distinct suburb or district. These are designated as 'in' the relevant town or city which is enclosed in square brackets, e.g. Knowle [in Bristol].

b. Places absorbed into urban development, as above, but of which the name has not survived as that of a distinct suburb or district. These are designated as 'in' the relevant town or city in square brackets, also as above, but the place-name is enclosed within single inverted commas, e.g. 'Tessall' [in Birmingham].

c. Places now lost underwater have their names enclosed in single inverted commas and are followed by an indication of their former whereabouts in square brackets if known, e.g. 'Syndercombe' [in Clatworthy Reservoir].

d. Names of places lost in rural areas are enclosed in single or double inverted commas as set out in 3 and 4 above. However, they may also be designated as being 'in' the parish to which they belonged when this is known. e.g. "Sortelai" [in Quainton], 'Ashden' [in Compton].

e. Those lost places which can be reliably located have been plotted on the accompanying county map. Those which can only be approximately located are included in the Index and the translation but are not mapped.

13. Use of names other than Domesday derivatives

All modern names used in this edition are derived from those of 1086 with only the following exceptions:

a. Where the name of the Domesday Book estate has been entirely superseded by a more recent name that covers the same extent, e.g. Reigate (Surrey) for 'Churchfield'; Padstow (Corn.) for *Lanweneboc*.

b. Where the later name of the Domesday Book estate is derived from the TRE or TRW holder or his title, e.g. Dodington (Som.) for 'Stowey'; Bishopstone (Herefs.) for 'Mansell'.

c. Where it is now possible to identify places which were sited along the banks of a river and which bear only the river name in Domesday Book, as with many settlements on the Ottery (Devon) and the Piddle (Dorset).

d. Where the holding is un-named in Domesday Book, but its name can be reliably established from any other contemporary documents, such as those mentioned in the introduction to these notes above.

PLACE-NAMES IN DOMESDAY BOOK (*ITALIC TYPE*)

14. Variant forms

All variant forms found in these county folios of Domesday Book are indexed.

15. Abbreviation

Place-names that are specifically shortened in the MS with abbreviation-marks are given in their extended form.

OTHER

16. Use of *u*, *v*, *w*

Since *u* and *v* are used indiscriminately in this MS, as in others of the period, they are here transposed to be closest to the modern spelling of the place-names. Double-*u* (*uu*) is always transposed as *w*, except in names enclosed in double inverted commas (see 3 above) where the scribe's original orthography is maintained.

17. Use of hyphenated endings

Where the spelling of a name varies only by the addition of a final letter or letters, the shorter version is given followed by the variant ending after a hyphen. Thus *Evelai*, *Evelaia* appears as *Evelai-a*; *Heiford*, *Heiforde* as *Heiford-e*; *Winewic*, *Winewiche* as *Winewic-he*.

18. Page and folio references

References to the pages of editorial matter in this volume are printed in **bold**, and are followed by the references to the folio numbers of the facsimile and the translation, which are identical for both.

19. Recto and Verso

Folio numbers without suffix indicate the *recto* of the folio, while suffix 'v' indicates the *verso*.

20. Use of ‡

A double-dagger ‡ before a main entry refers to the errata section printed at the end of these indices, if such is required.

SURREY

EDITOR'S NOTES

'[London]' after a name in this index indicates places which since 1965 have lain within the administrative boundaries of Greater London.

In the continuous-tone process of reproduction employed for the facsimile, certain problems of definition arise where the red of the rubrication is either contiguous with or superimposed over the dark browns of the lettering. Very occasionally this association of colours causes slight distortions to the capitals of the place-names which were normally through-lined in red, and can result in an apparent misreading. Accordingly, in order to resolve any doubt, every place-name has been checked against the manuscript itself and the following readings are thereby confirmed:

Modern name, folio number, column and ● counted from top	in the facsimile could be read as:	confirmed from the manuscript as
EGHAM, 32 right, 10th ●	COEHAM	EGEHAM
[?] LOLLESWORTH, 36v right, bottom ●	LaDESORDE	LODESORDE
MICKLEHAM, 32 left, 1st ●	MIOLEHAM	MICLEHAM

INDEX OF PERSONS AND ECCLESIASTICAL BODIES

NOTES

1. TRE, TRW

Most of the entries in Domesday Book record two distinct categories of landholder: those English or Anglo-Scandinavian owners who held land before the Conquest (TRE, *tempore regis Edwardi*, 'in the time of King Edward'), and those who dispossessed them after 1066 (TRW, *tempore regis Willelmi,* 'in the time of King William')—or more particularly twenty years later at the time of the Conqueror's survey. It is usual for the Church to maintain continuity of ownership throughout both periods, but it is rare for an individual to do so. Since Domesday Book is a description of the situation at the time of its compilation in 1086–7, the circumstances obtaining TRE are invariably entered in the past tense, TRW in the present.

2. Use of * †

Prefixed asterisks * indicate references to the names of English or Anglo-Scandinavian landholders or churches mentioned only in a TRE context. Daggers † signify those which are stated to have continued their tenancy from the TRE to the TRW period. Names found only TRW have no prefixed symbol.

3. The Kings

The references to King Edward and to King William are divided for convenience into categories which encompass various aspects of kingship. The references to King Edward implied by the abbreviation TRE are not indexed. Where the text shows that someone in the TRE period *tenuit de rege Edwardo*, 'held of King Edward', the references are indexed under the category of King Edward 'as lord'.

References to the equivalent TRW phrase *tenet de rege*, 'holds of the king', are not indexed as it was not used systematically and was anyway superfluous because in feudal theory current after the Conquest all land was technically held of the king.

4. Abbeys and Churches

The terms *Abbatia,* 'Abbey', and *Æcclesia,* 'Church' are sometimes used interchangeably in Domesday Book for large monastic institutions. In this index, irrespective of text, 'Abbey' is always used for the Benedictine houses, both in England and on the continent, while 'Church' is reserved for secular houses, i.e. colleges of priests, non-monastic bishoprics, minsters, etc. Only churches recorded as owning land are indexed here.

5. Personal Names TRE

All TRE names are standardized in accordance with O. von Feilitzen, *The Pre-Conquest Personal Names of Domesday Book* (Uppsala, 1937) with the following exceptions: Alfred, Edgar, Edith, Edmund, Edward, Edwin, Harold, Morcar, Siward, Stigand, Swein and Waltheof.

Old English forms are used in preference to Scandinavian variants. When no Old English form is attested, names are standardized first to their Anglo-Scandinavian, then to their Old Danish, Old Swedish, and finally Old Norse forms.

6. Personal Names TRW

There is no authority equivalent to von Feilitzen for TRW names, and their transposition into modern forms by individual historians has seldom been consistent. For this edition the editors have retained what they perceive to have become the 'accepted' forms of certain names despite inconsistencies. Thus, for example, *Albertus Lotharingensis* becomes Albert of Lorraine, not the Lotharingian, whilst *Walterius Flandrensis* remains Walter the Fleming, not of Flanders, in the style used for most non-Norman continentals. However, a policy of standardization has been established for the aspects of nomenclature which follow.

Modern anglicized forms of Christian names are preferred, e.g. Gilbert for *Giselbertus*, Geoffrey for *Goisfridus,* Hugh for *Hugo*, Ralph for *Radulfus*.

Continental and English toponymics appear in the modern form of the place-name e.g. Robert d'Oilly not *Robert de Oilgi*, Roger of Westerham not *Roger de Oisteram*. As in these examples, 'de' is used for continental places of origin, 'of' for English names.

Continental patronymics are expressed with the prefix 'fitz', e.g. Hugh fitzBaldric. The equivalent English or Anglo-Scandinavian names are expressed as 'son of', e.g. Swein son of Azur. This rule is also applied to patronymics in TRE names.

Ambiguous TRW personal names which are attested in both Anglo-Scandinavian and Continental sources are given their Continental forms unless the manuscript specifically identifies any person so named as English.

TRW names with obscure Latin forms or with no modern equivalent appear in the Index as they do in the manuscript, but without the *-us* ending, e.g. Otbert for *Otbertus*, Winemar for *Winemarus*.

7. Titles

Main entries are indexed under the toponymic, and the personal name(s), where known, are supplied in square brackets, e.g. Mortain, [Robert], Count of; Coutances, [Geoffrey de Mowbray], Bishop of. If these name(s) occur explicitly in the folios of this country, the square brackets are left off.

8. Occupational Names

Examples: Alwine the huntsman, Gilbert the cook, Regenbald the priest. Although Domesday Book describes many of these persons with other descriptive suffixes—for instance Regenbald occurs variously in different counties as 'the priest', 'the chaplain', 'the king's chaplain', and 'of Cirencester'—only that or those which occur in the folios of this particular county are listed here.

9. Cross-indexing

All patronymics, non-titular toponymics, rank-names, bynames and occupational names are cross-indexed with the main entry under the Christian name. Examples:

Main Entry	Cross-reference
Eudo fitzHubert	Hubert, *see* Eudo fitzHubert
Alvred of Lincoln	Lincoln, *see* Alvred of Lincoln
Leofwine Cild	Cild, *see* Leofwine Cild
Alwine Cobbold	Cobbold, *see* Alwine Cobbold
Gilbert the cook	cook, *see* Gilbert the cook

In the case of Abbeys, main entries will be found under the place-name with the dedication cross-indexed: Ramsey, Abbey of St Benedict (main entry); St Benedict, Ramsey, Abbey of.

Secular churches are indexed under Church with a cross-reference to the dedication, and also to the place-name: Church of Saint-Remy of Rheims (main entry); Saint-Remy of Rheims, Church of; Rheims, Church of Saint-Remy of.

10. Folio References

Only one reference to a name is indexed per folio. The frequent use of *idem*, 'the same man', is not indexed as the name itself is not present. References are linked by a hyphen when the consecutive entries for a holder's fief cover more than one folio.

Folio numbers without suffix indicate the recto of the folio, while suffix 'v' indicates the verso.

SURREY

TRANSLATION

TRANSLATION

NOTES TO THE TRANSLATION

SOURCE AND STANDARDIZATION

THE translations in the County Edition of Domesday Book are based in the main upon those that appear in the *Victoria Histories of the Counties of England*, of which publication commenced in 1900 and is still in progress. The translator of the relevant county folios of Domesday Book in volume one of *VCH Surrey* (1902) was H. E. Malden. Alecto Historical Editions are grateful to the publishers of *VCH* for permission to make use of this translation.

In order that the translations contained in each of the county volumes can be served by a common system of indices, the text of all sources has been standardized so that place- and personal names as well as technical terms and certain common phrases are consistent throughout. The opportunity has also been taken to correct such errors as may have become apparent as a result of subsequent research.

For a detailed statement of the policies governing the treatment of names, see the notes which precede the 'Index of Places' and the 'Index of Persons and Ecclesiastical Bodies' above.

METHODS OF RELATING THE TRANSLATION TO THE FACSIMILE

Throughout the folios of Great Domesday Book there is considerable variation in the number of lines written per page, in the depth and width of the columns, and in the spaces that separate the numbered chapters. In order to assist the use of the facsimile and this translation together, the type-size and the lay-out of the pages of the translation have been designed to match the configuration of the MS text as closely as possible.

The MS was foliated in the seventeenth century on only the *recto* side of each page. In the translation the *verso* is also foliated with the number followed by v.

● to the left, within the column, signifies the presence of one of the larger rubricated initial letters that commonly begin each entry. This device is provided to enable the reader more easily to relate passages in the translation to those in the facsimile by counting the spots on the former against the more prominent initials in the latter.

TYPOGRAPHY

Roman type is reserved for the original text of Great Domesday, including all corrections and marginal additions made to the MS at the time of its compilation in the late eleventh century.

Italic type is used for all matter added subsequently during the Middle Ages and up to recent times.

The use of upper and lower case is the same as in the MS:

FULL CAPITALS represent the large rustic capitals used for county- and chapter-headings, which are all written in red.

LARGE AND SMALL CAPITALS represent matter written in black rustic capitals within the text and usually through-lined in red. Those not written in capitals, whether intentionally or in error, are here transposed in lower case.

MARGINALIA

The translations of those passages entirely written in the margin are printed as close as is possible to the position they occupy in the MS, in smaller type where necessary. A complete key to the system of symbols employed here for the marginal notes and signs found in the MS, such as § for the transposition signs, M, B, S, etc. preceding ● in certain counties, and [1], [2], [3], □, ⬚, ☒, etc., is given in Appendix I, 'The Marginalia of Great Domesday Book', in the associated *Domesday Book Studies* volume, pp. 160–2.

EDITORIAL CONVENTIONS

Square brackets are reserved for editorial insertions.

[*sic*] — indicates a scribal error in the MS, here reproduced in the translation. The only exception is incorrect chapter numbering.

[. . .] — signifies a gap in the MS text, either left blank by the scribe for an insertion to be added later, or as a result of erasure. Three full points within the brackets are the standard length in the translations regardless of the actual extent of the gap in the MS.

† 7 hides † — Daggers enclose the tentative translation of a passage, phrase or numeral which is obscure in the MS, owing either to slips of the pen, to unclear alteration by the scribe, or to the worn condition of the parchment.

<u>7 hides</u> — Underlining indicated words or passages marked for deletion in the MS: the same convention is followed in the translation where no correction has been added suprascript. In the latter case, only the corrected text is given.

|it is worth 12*s*.| — Bars within the text enclose the full extent of a passage of which part is written in the margin, where a note will be found to that effect in square brackets.

[?]WESTON — The modern equivalent given for a Domesday place-name which is probable, but not certain.

[?Weston] — A place left unnamed in Domesday Book, but which can be tentatively identified from internal evidence or from the evidence of other related documents.

WESTON [in Parishbrook] — Where a county contains two or more modern places with the same name, they are differentiated by indicating the parish 'in' which each of them lies.

WESTON [near Oldborough] — In the above instance, when one of the place-names is the same or partially the same as the name of the parish in which it lies, giving the awkward WESTON [in Weston], its situation is instead indicated as being 'near' a prominent town or feature.

[Great or Little] WESTON — The use of 'or' indicates that it is uncertain which of two or more modern places now represent the Domesday place-name, or whether all did so.

[Great and Little] WESTON — The use of 'and' indicates that two or more modern places lie within the territory of the same Domesday estate.

WESTON [OXON.] — County abbreviations indicate that a locality recorded in the folios of this county lies within the boundaries of another in modern times. Throughout this edition the modern county boundaries are taken to be those that obtained prior to the restructuring of the counties in 1974.

NOTES TO THE TRANSLATION

Use of Inverted Commas

"CELVERDESCOTE" Double inverted commas indicate a place-name found only in Domesday Book and for which there is no known later equivalent, or of which the form may be corrupt.

Hundred- and wapentake-names are similarly treated, but a typical form is used if there are variants.

'SCULTHORP' Single inverted commas indicate the latest or most typical known form of a name which remained in use beyond the eleventh century, but which either has not survived into modern times at all, or which only appears on twentieth-century maps as the name of a feature such as a river, hill, wood, etc., rather than as a place of habitation. This also applies to names without a continuous history and which have only recently been revived for antiquarian reasons.

Hundred- and wapentake-names which are antiquarian revivals are similarly treated. Single inverted commas also indicate such names derived from places which had disappeared before the compilation of the first OS one-inch maps in the early nineteenth century, either because they never were the names of inhabited communities, or because they had fallen into disuse by that time. In such cases the name-form adopted is the latest, most or a regularized form.

EDITOR'S NOTE

In the initial list of tenants-in-chief on f.30 the chapter numbered XXXIII is allotted to Reginald fitzErchenbald who does not in fact hold any land in Surrey as tenant-in-chief. On f.36v, where the chapter occurs, the holder is stated to be Alvred of Marlborough and Reginald his sub-tenant. This discrepancy is noted here only and is not signalled by [*sic*] in the translation.

HERE ARE NOTED THE LANDHOLDERS IN SURREY

THE LAND OF THE KING

IN WOKING HUNDRED

• IN GUILDFORD KING WILLIAM HAS 75 closes in which dwell 175 men. TRE it rendered £18. 0*s.* 3*d.*; now it is valued at £30, and yet it renders £32.

Of the aforesaid closes, Ranulph the clerk has 3 closes in which 6 men dwell, and of these the same Ranulph has sake and soke unless the common geld from which no one may escape be laid upon the vill. If his man commits an offence in the vill, and, after being distrained, escapes, the king's reeve has nothing from him. But if he is accused and is distrained there, then the king has the fine. Archbishop Stigand held these [closes] thus.

Ranulph the sheriff holds 1 close, which he has up to this time held of the Bishop of Bayeux. The men, however, testify that it does not belong to any manor, but that he who held it TRE granted it to Tovi, the reeve of the vill, in compensation for a forfeiture of his.

There is another house which the reeve of the Bishop of Bayeux holds of the manor of Bramley. Concerning this the men of the shire say that he has no other right there, except that the reeve of the vill married a certain widow whose house it was, and therefore the bishop put that house into his own manor, and the king has hitherto lost the customary dues, but the bishop has them.

The jurors declare also concerning another house that it belongs to Bramley, only because the reeve of this vill was a friend of that man who had this house, and, on his [friend's] death, transferred it to the manor of Bramley.

Waleran also disseised a certain man of a house from which King Edward had the customary dues. Now Odbert holds it with the customary dues, as he says, by [grant from] King William.

Robert de Watteville holds 1 house, which rendered every customary due TRE; now it renders nothing.

• King William holds in demesne WOKING. It was [part] of King Edward's farm. It was then assessed at 15½ hides. They have never paid geld. There is land for 6 ploughs. In demesne is 1 [plough]; and 33 villans and 9 bordars with 20 ploughs. There is a church. Osbern holds it. And there is 1 mill rendering 11*s.* 4*d.* There are 32 acres of meadow, [and] woodland for 133 pigs.

Of this land, Walter fitzOther holds 3 virgates. A certain forester held this TRE, and it was then put out of the manor by King Edward. Now there is nothing.

TRE, and afterwards, it was worth £15 by tale; now £15 by weight, and 25*s.* to the sheriff.

• The king holds in demesne STOKE [in Guildford]. It was [part] of King Edward's farm. It was then assessed at 17 hides. They have paid no geld. There is land for 16 ploughs. In demesne are 2 ploughs; and 24 villans and 10 bordars with 20 ploughs. There is a church which William holds of the king, with half a hide in alms. There are 5 slaves, and 2 mills rendering 25*s.*, and 16 acres of meadow. [There is] woodland for 40 pigs, and this is in the king's park. TRE, and afterwards, it was worth £12; now £15, yet he who holds it pays £15 by weight. The sheriff has 25*s.*

IN BRIXTON HUNDRED

• The king holds BERMONDSEY. Earl Harold held it. It was then assessed at 13 hides; now at 12 hides. There is land for 8 ploughs. In demesne is 1 plough; and 25 villans and 33 bordars with 4 ploughs. There is a new and handsome church, and 20 acres of meadow. [There is] woodland for 5 pigs as pannage. In London, 13 burgesses paying 44*d.* TRE, as now, worth £15; and the sheriff has 20*s.* The Count of Mortain holds 1 hide, which, TRE and afterwards, was in this manor.

• The king holds MERTON. Earl Harold held it. It was then assessed, as now, at 20 hides. There is land for 21 ploughs. In demesne are 2 ploughs; and 56 villans and 13 bordars with 18 ploughs. There is a church, and 2 mills rendering 60*s.*, and 10 acres of meadow, [and] woodland for 80 pigs. TRE it was worth £25; and afterwards £16; now £35, yet he who holds it pays £43. In Southwark 16 messuages rendering 18*s.* 2*d.* belong to this manor.

A certain Urk holds 2 hides, which always belonged in this manor, and are in another hundred. He himself held them TRE. It was then assessed at 2 hides; now at nothing. There is 1 plough in demesne, and 2 acres of meadow. It has always been worth 20*s.*

• The Bishop of Lisieux holds in Kent 2 sulungs which belonged to this manor TRE and [in the time] of King William, as the men of the hundred testify. He himself calls to warranty the Bishop of Bayeux, and his reeve has not wanted to plead concerning it.

IN WALLINGTON HUNDRED

• The king holds in demesne WALLINGTON. TRE, as now, it was assessed at 11 hides. There is land for 11 ploughs. In demesne is 1 plough; and 15 villans and 14 bordars with 10 ploughs. There are 3 slaves, and 2 mills rendering 30*s.*, and 8 acres of meadow. [There is] woodland which is in Kent.

Richard of Tonbridge holds of this manor 1 virgate, with woodland, from which he evicted a peasant who dwelt there. Now it renders to the sheriff 10*s.* a year. The whole manor TRE was worth £15; now £10.

IN REIGATE HUNDRED

• The king holds in demesne REIGATE. Queen Edith held it. It was then assessed at 37½ hides; now for the king's use at 34 hides. There is land [. . .]. In demesne are 3 ploughs; and 67 villans and 11 bordars with 26 ploughs. There are 2 mills rendering 12*s.* less 2*d.*, and 12 acres of meadow. [There is] woodland for 140 pigs as pannage, and from the herbage, 43 pigs. It is now valued at £40, and renders as much.

In Kingston Hundred

• The king holds in demesne KINGSTON UPON THAMES. It was [part] of King Edward's farm. It was then assessed at 39 hides; now at nothing. There is land for 32 ploughs. In demesne are 2 ploughs; and 86 villans and 14 bordars with 25 ploughs. There is a church, and 2 slaves, and 5 mills rendering 20*s.*, and 2 fisheries rendering 10*s.*, and a third fishery very good but without rent. There are 40 acres of meadow, [and] woodland for 6 pigs. TRE and afterwards, as now, worth £30.

Of the villans of this vill, Humphrey the chamberlain had, and has, 1 villan in his charge for the purpose of collecting the queen's wool. He also received from this man 20*s.* as a relief when his father was dead.

In 'Copthorne' Hundred

• The king holds in demesne EWELL. TRE it was assessed at 16 hides less 1 virgate; now at $13\frac{1}{2}$ hides at farm. There is land [. . .]. In demesne is 1 plough; and 48 villans and 4 bordars with 15 ploughs. There are 2 mills rendering 10*s.*, and 14 acres of meadow. [There is] woodland for 100 pigs. From the herbage, 11 pigs. TRE it was worth £20; and afterwards, as now, £16; and yet it renders £25. The men of the hundred testify that 2 hides and 1 virgate have been subtracted from this manor, which were there TRE; but the reeves let them out to their friends, and a woodland dene and a croft. The church of Leatherhead belongs to this manor, with 40 acres of land. It is worth 20*s.* Osbern de Eu holds it.

• The king holds in demesne FETCHAM. Queen Edith held it. It was then assessed at 7 hides; now at none. There is land [. . .]. In demesne is half a plough and 2 oxen; and 3 villans and 10 bordars with 2 ploughs. There are 4 mills rendering 4*s.*, and 10 acres of meadow. From the pannage and herbage, 6 pigs. TRE, and afterwards, it was worth 60*s.*; now 50*s.*

In Blackheath Hundred

• The king holds in demesne GOMSHALL. Earl Harold held it. It was then assessed at 20 hides; now at nothing. There is land for 20 ploughs. In demesne are 2 [ploughs]; and 30 villans and 8 bordars with 18 ploughs. There are 6 slaves, and a mill rendering 40*d.*, and 3 acres of meadow, [and] woodland for 30 pigs. TRE it was worth £15; and afterwards £10; now £20, and yet it renders £30. The villans of this vill are quit of every sheriff's matter. Of the land of this manor, the bishop put half a hide in the manor of Bramley wrongfully, and holds it, which had been in Gomshall TRE, and also [in the time] of [King] William.

In WOTTON Hundred the king has in demesne 1 hide, which belongs to Gomshall.

• The king holds in demesne SHERE. Queen Edith held it. It was then assessed at 9 hides, and yet there were then 16 hides there. Recently it has not paid geld. There is land for 14 ploughs. In demesne are 2 ploughs; and 19 villans and 6 bordars with 12 ploughs. There is a church, and 6 slaves, and 2 mills rendering 10*s.*, and 3 acres of meadow, [and] woodland for 50 pigs. TRE and afterwards, as now, worth £15.

In WOTTON Hundred the king has in demesne 3 virgates, which belong to Shere and are valued there.

In Wotton Hundred

• The king holds in demesne DORKING. Queen Edith held it. It was then assessed at $10\frac{1}{2}$ hides; now at nothing. There is land for 14 ploughs. In demesne are 2 ploughs; and 38 villans and 13 bordars with 14 ploughs. There is a church, and 4 slaves, and 3 mills rendering 15*s.* 4*d.* There are 3 acres of meadow. [There is] woodland for 50 pigs as pannage. From the herbage, 38 pigs. TRE and afterwards, as now, worth £18.

A certain Eadric, who held this manor, gave 2 hides to his daughters and they could go where they would with their lands. Of these hides, Richard of Tonbridge has 1, which does not belong to any manor, and he has there in demesne 1 plough, with 1 bordar, and a mill at the hall, and [there is] 1 acre of meadow. Herfrid holds the other hide of the Bishop of Bayeux. Richard's hide is worth 20*s.*, Herfrid's 10*s.*

From the 3 manors which Queen Edith had in Surrey, the sheriff has £7, because he affords them aid when they have need.

In Godalming Hundred

• The king holds in demesne GODALMING. King Edward held it. Then [there were] 24 hides. They have never paid geld. There is land for 30 ploughs. In demesne are 3 ploughs; and 50 villans and 29 bordars with 19 ploughs. There are 2 slaves, and 3 mills rendering 41*s.* 8*d.*, and 25 acres of meadow, [and] woodland for 100 pigs. TRE it was worth £25; and afterwards ⊠ £20; now £30 by tale, and yet it renders £30 weighed and assayed.

Ranulph Flambard holds of this manor a church, to which belong 3 hides. Wulfmær held it of King Edward. They have never paid geld. There is land for 2 ploughs. In demesne is 1 [plough]; and 5 villans and 12 cottars with 2 ploughs. There are 15 acres of meadow, and woodland for 3 pigs.

The same Ranulph holds another church in the same place, which renders 12*s.* a year. These 3 hides TRE, as now, were worth £4; when received, £3.

• The same Ranulph holds of the king TUESLEY. It belonged to Godalming. Leofwine held it of King Edward. Then, as now, [there was] 1 hide. It does not pay geld. There is land for 1 plough, and there is [1 plough], with 1 villan and 6 cottars and 1 slave. TRE it was worth 60*s.*; and afterwards, as now, 40*s.*

• In 'ELMBRIDGE' [Hundred] Ealdgyth, a certain woman, holds of the king 1 virgate. It is worth 3*s.*

II. THE LAND OF THE ARCHBISHOP OF CANTERBURY

In Wallington Hundred

• ARCHBISHOP Lanfranc holds in demesne CROYDON. TRE it was assessed at 80 hides, and now at 16 hides and 1 virgate. There is land for 20 ploughs. In demesne are 4 ploughs; and 48 villans and 25 bordars with 34 ploughs. There is a church, and a mill rendering 5*s.*, and 8 acres of meadow, [and] woodland for 200 pigs.

Of the land of this manor, Restold holds 7 hides of the archbishop; Ralph 1 hide; and they have £7. 8*s.* from them for rent. TRE, and afterwards, the whole was worth £12; now £27 to the archbishop, £10. 10*s.* to his men.

7 • The archbishop himself holds CHEAM for the sustenance of the monks. TRE it was assessed at 20 hides, and now at 4 hides. There is land for 14 ploughs. In demesne are 2 ploughs; and 25 villans and 12 cottars with 15 ploughs. There is a church, and 5 slaves, and 1 acre of meadow, [and] woodland for 25 pigs. TRE, and afterwards, it was worth £8; now £14.

In Brixton Hundred

⊠ • The archbishop himself holds in demesne MORTLAKE. TRE it was assessed at 80 hides. The canons of St Paul's hold 8 of these hides, which with these [others] have paid, and do pay, geld. Now they pay geld for 25 hides all together. There is land for 35 ploughs. In demesne are 5 ploughs; and 80 villans and 14 bordars with 28 ploughs. There is a church, and 16 slaves, and 2 mills rendering 100*s.*, and 20 acres of meadow. From the woodland, 55 pigs as pannage.

In London were 17 messuages rendering 52*d.* In Southwark, 4 messuages rendering 27*d.*, and 20*s.* from the toll of the vill of Putney, and a fishery without rent. This fishery belonged to

Earl Harold in Mortlake TRE, and Archbishop Stigand had it a long while TRW; and yet they say that Harold set it up by force TRE in the land of Kingston upon Thames and in the land of St Paul's. The whole manor TRE was worth £32; and afterwards £10; now £38.

• Baynard holds of the archbishop WALWORTH. TRE it was for the clothing of the monks. It was then [. . .] assessed at 5 hides; now at 3½ hides. There is land for 3 ploughs. In demesne is 1 plough; and 14 villans and 5 bordars with 3 ploughs. There is a church, and 8 acres of meadow. TRE it was worth 30*s*.; and afterwards 20*s*.; now 60*s*.

IN REIGATE HUNDRED

• The archbishop himself holds MERSTHAM [Merstham and South Merstham] for the clothing of the monks. TRE it was assessed at 20 hides; now at 5 hides. There is land for 8 ploughs. In demesne are 2 ploughs; and 21 villans and 4 bordars with 8 ploughs. There is a church, and a mill rendering 30*d*., and 8 slaves, and 8 acres of meadow. [There is] woodland for 5 pigs. From the herbage, 16 pigs. TRE it was worth £8; and afterwards £4; now £12.

IN WOKING HUNDRED

The archbishop himself holds EAST HORSLEY for the sustenance of the monks. TRE it was assessed at 14 hides; now at 3 hides and 1½ virgates. There is land for 5 ploughs. In demesne is 1 [plough]; and 13 villans and 6 bordars with 1½ ploughs. There are 3 slaves. [There is] woodland for 50 pigs. TRE it was worth £4; and afterwards the same; now as much, and yet it renders 100*s*.

II. THE LAND OF THE BISHOP OF WINCHESTER

THE BISHOP OF WINCHESTER holds FARNHAM. ST PETER always held it. TRE it was assessed at 60 hides, and now at 40 hides. There is land [. . .]. In demesne are 5 ploughs; and 36 villans and 11 bordars with 29 ploughs. There are 11 slaves, and 6 mills rendering 46*s*. 4*d*., and 35 acres of meadow, [and] woodland for 150½ pigs as pannage. Of the land of this manor Ralph holds of the bishop 4 hides less 1 virgate; William 3 hides and 1 virgate; Wazo half a hide. In these lands [are] 3 ploughs in demesne; and 22 villans and 9 bordars with 6 ploughs. [There is] woodland for 25 pigs. TRE the manor, so far as it lies in Surrey, was worth £55; when received, £30; now the demesne of the bishop [is worth] £38, [the land] of his men £9. Osbern de Eu holds the church of this manor of the bishop. It is worth £6, with 1 hide, which he has in Hampshire.

III. THE LAND OF BISHOP OSBERN

IN WOKING HUNDRED

• Bishop OSBERN holds WOKING. He himself held it TRE, and it was then assessed at 8 hides; now at 3½ hides. There is land for 9½ ploughs. In demesne [are] 1½ ploughs; and 20 villans and 6 bordars with 8½ ploughs. There are 3 slaves, and a mill rendering 30*d*., and 14 acres of meadow, [and] woodland for 28 pigs.

• This manor has, and had, a customary due in the king's woodland of Woking; it is this: that the lord of this vill can have in this woodland 120 pigs without [payment for] pannage. 2 men, Ansgot and Godfrey, hold this manor of the bishop; each [holds] 4 hides. The whole, TRE and afterwards, was worth £10; now £9. 10*s*.

• The bishop himself holds TYTING. Almær the huntsman held it TRE. It was then assessed at 1 hide; and the same now. There is land for 2 ploughs. In demesne is 1 plough; and 1 villan and 6 bordars with 1 plough. TRE, and afterwards, it was worth £3; now 40*s*. The men of the hundred testify that this manor was leased through the sheriff out of King Edward's farm, and that Bishop Osbern did not have this manor TRE.

7 V. THE LAND OF THE BISHOP OF BAYEUX

IN BLACKHEATH HUNDRED

• The Bishop of BAYEUX holds in demesne BRAMLEY. Æthelnoth Cild held it of King Edward. It was then assessed at 34 hides. 4 of these hides belonged to free men who could withdraw from Æthelnoth. Over and above these is land for 2 ploughs in the manor itself which never have rendered geld. All these lands are now in the farm of Bramley. There is land for 35 ploughs. In demesne are 6 ploughs; and 84 villans and 40 cottars with 32 ploughs. There are 3 churches, and 18 slaves, and 5 mills rendering 26*s*., and 20 acres of meadow, [and] woodland for 100 pigs. TRE it was worth £40; and afterwards £30; now £60, and yet it renders £80 less 40*d*. Since the bishop was seised [of it] it has not paid geld. 2

• The bishop himself holds CHILWORTH in Bramley. Alwine Boy held it, and could go where he would. It was then assessed at 3 hides; now at nothing. There is land [. . .]. In demesne is 1 plough; and 6 villans and 2 cottars with 2 ploughs. There is a mill rendering 7*s*. The whole is worth 70*s*. 2

In BRAMLEY there are 2 more hides. Eskil held them TRE, and could go where he would. It was then assessed at 2 hides;
2 now at nothing. There are 3 villans and 1 cottar with 1 plough. There is land for 1 plough. It is worth 36*s*.

The bishop has 2½ more hides in the same place, which Ælfric held TRE, and could go with them where he would. There is land for 2 ploughs. It lies in Wotton Hundred. It is worth 32*s*.

The same bishop has 1 more hide there. A certain widow holds it, and held it TRE, and could go where she would. It was then assessed at 1 hide; now at nothing. It is worth 10*s*.

IN BLACKHEATH HUNDRED

• The bishop himself has in demesne 3 hides. Alweard held these, and could go where he would with them. There are 5 villans and 8 cottars with 2 ploughs. There are 5 slaves, and a mill rendering 20*d*. The whole is worth 100*s*. a year.

• The bishop himself has in this hundred land for 1 plough. Alwine held it TRE. It is worth 30*s*. Then [. . .].

All the land that belongs to Bramley has not paid geld since the bishop received it.

IN GODALMING HUNDRED

• The bishop himself holds in demesne RODSALL. Tovi held it TRE, and could go with it where he would. It was then assessed at 5 hides; now at nothing. There is land for 2 ploughs. There are 3 villans and 4 cottars with 1 plough, and 2 acres of meadow. [There is] woodland for 4 pigs. TRE and afterwards, as now, worth 40*s*.

• The bishop himself holds in demesne FARNCOMBE. Asgot held it TRE, and could go with it where he would. It was then assessed at 3½ hides; now at nothing. There is land for 2 ploughs. There are 8 villans and 3 cottars with 2 ploughs, and 15 acres of meadow. [There is] woodland for 3 pigs. It is and was worth 24*s*. A certain reeve of the king, named Lufa, claims this manor, and the men of the hundred bear witness for him, that he was holding it of the king when the king was in Wales, and he afterwards held it until the Bishop of Bayeux arrived in Kent. The bishop himself has transferred Rodsall and Farncombe to the farm of Bramley.

IN TANDRIDGE HUNDRED

• Ansketil de Rots holds of the bishop TATSFIELD. Ælfric held it of King Edward. Then, as now, it was assessed at half a hide. There is land [. . .]. In demesne is 1 plough; and 5 villans and 9 bordars with 1 plough. There are 12 slaves. TRE it was worth 30*s*.; and afterwards 40*s*.; now 60[*s*.].

• Hugh holds of the bishop a manor which Cana held of King Edward. It was then assessed at 4 hides; now at half [a hide]. There is land for 4 ploughs. In demesne is 1 plough, and 5 villans and 2 bordars. TRE it was worth £4; and afterwards 20*s*.; now 40*s*.

IN WALLINGTON HUNDRED

• The canons of Bayeux hold of the bishop MITCHAM for 5 hides. Beorhtric held it of King Edward. He himself had 6½ hides, but Odbert holds 1, which his predecessor held in pledge of Beorhtric for half a mark of gold.

In the land of the canons are 4 villans and 1 cottar with 2 ploughs and 1 slave, and 40 acres of meadow. There is land for 2 ploughs. It is and was worth 40*s*.

In Odbert's land are 4 acres of meadow. They are worth 7*s*. [There is] nothing more. Ansgot holds half a hide of the bishop. It is worth 5*s*.

In this manor the canons themselves hold of the bishop 2½ hides, which 2 men held of King Edward. There is 1 plough in demesne; with 1 villan and 2 bordars and 1 slave, and half a plough, and 12 acres of meadow. [It has] always [been worth] 20*s*.

• The canons themselves hold of the bishop 'WHITFORD' [in Mitcham]. Eadmær held it of King Edward. Then, as now, it was assessed at 3 hides. There is land for 2 ploughs. In demesne is 1 plough; and 2 villans and 6 cottars with 2 ploughs, and 4 acres of meadow. TRE, as now, worth 30*s*.; when received, 10*s*.

☒ • Richard holds of the bishop BANSTEAD. Alnoth held it of King Edward. It was then assessed at 29 hides; now at 9½ hides. There is land for 16 ploughs. In demesne are 2 ploughs; and 28 villans and 15 cottars with 15 ploughs. There is a church, and 7 slaves, and a mill rendering 20*s*. [There is] woodland for 20 pigs, and in Southwark 1 house rendering 40*d*. belongs to this manor, and in London Alnoth had a demesne messuage belonging to this manor. Adam fitzHubert now holds it of the bishop. The whole manor TRE was worth £10; and afterwards 100*s*.; now £8. Of the land of this manor, Geoffrey holds of Richard 5 hides, Ralph 2 hides, [and] Wulfsige 2 hides. The whole is worth £6. 10*s*.

• The same Ralph holds of the bishop CHALDON. Deoring held it of King Edward. Then, as now, it was assessed at 2 hides. There is land for 2 ploughs, and there are [2 ploughs] in demesne, and a church. TRE it was worth 40*s*.; and afterwards 20*s*.; now £4.

IN BRIXTON HUNDRED

• The Bishop of Lisieux holds of the bishop HATCHAM. Beorhtsige held it of King Edward. Then, as now, it was assessed at 3 hides. There is land for 3 ploughs. There are 9 villans and 2 bordars with 3 ploughs; and there are 6 acres of meadow, [and] woodland for 3 pigs. TRE and afterwards, as now, worth 40*s*.

IN REIGATE HUNDRED

• Herfrid holds of the bishop GATTON. Earl Leofwine held it. It was then assessed at 10 hides; now at 2½ hides. There is land for 5 ploughs.

In demesne are 2 ploughs; and 6 villans and 3 bordars with 2 ploughs. There is a church, and 6 acres of meadow, [and] woodland and herbage for 7 pigs. TRE, as now, worth £6; when received, £3.

• Ansgot holds of the bishop half a hide in Wallington Hundred. Øpi held this TRE, and could go where he would. It is worth 5*s*.

IN BRIXTON HUNDRED

• The Bishop of Lisieux holds of the bishop PECKHAM. Alflæd held it of Harold TRE, and it belonged to Battersea. Then, as now, it was assessed at 2 hides. There is land for 1 plough. There is 1 villan and 3 bordars, and 2 acres of meadow. TRE, as now, worth 30*s*.; when received, 20*s*.

• Ansgot holds of the bishop STREATHAM. Edwin held it TRE, and could go where he would. Then, as now, it was assessed at 1 hide. There is 1 plough, and 2 villans. It is and was worth 25*s*.

IN 'COPTHORNE' HUNDRED

• Hugh holds of the bishop PACHESHAM. Almær held it of the king TRE. It was then assessed at 4 hides; and now at 3 virgates. There is land [. . .]. In demesne are 2 ploughs; and 11 villans and 8 bordars with 2 ploughs. There are 4 slaves, and 2 halves of a mill rendering 12*s*., and 5 acres of meadow, [and] woodland for 3 pigs. TRE it was worth 40*s*.; and afterwards 20*s*.; now 70*s*.

• Ranulph holds of the bishop 1 hide and 1 virgate. Leofric held them of Harold, free, and could go where he would. This land is now assessed at 1 virgate. 2 villans have half a plough there. TRE [it was worth] 20*s*.; and afterwards 12[*s*.]; now 10*s*.

• Baynard holds of the bishop 1 hide, which Almær held of Earl Harold, and he could go where he pleased. It was then assessed at 1 hide; now at 1 virgate. In demesne is 1 plough, with 1 bordar, and half a mill rendering 6*s*. TRE it was worth 20*s*.; and afterwards 10*s*.; now 24*s*.

• In Wallington Hundred Adam fitzHubert has 1 hide of the bishop, which has never paid geld.

• The bishop himself holds CUDDINGTON. Earl Leofwine held it. It was then assessed at 30 hides. Of these, the earl held 20 hides; and the allodial tenants of the vill, who could withdraw with their lands where they would, held 10 hides. The bishop now holds 6 of these 10 with the other 20 [hides]. These 26 hides are now assessed at 5 hides. The bishop holds this as 1 manor. Ilbert now holds of the bishop these 26 hides. He himself [has] 22 hides, and 1 of his men 4 hides. In demesne is 1 plough; and 7 villans and 9 bordars with 6 ploughs. There are 4 slaves, and a mill rendering 40*d*.

Of these hides, Ralph holds 4 hides. Wulfwine holds of the king 1 hide and 3 parts of 1 hide. In demesne is 1 plough; and 4 villans and 4 bordars with 1 plough. The whole manor TRE was worth £11; and afterwards 100*s*.; now £9. 12*s*. Of the land of this manor, Restald holds 2 hides, but he renders account in Wallington Hundred.

• The canons hold ASHTEAD of the Bishop of Bayeux. Thorgisl held it of Earl Harold. It was then assessed at 9 hides; now at 3 hides and 1 virgate. There is land [. . .]. In demesne are 2 ploughs; and 33 villans and 11 bordars with 14 ploughs. There are 9 slaves, and 7 pigs from the herbage, and 4 acres of meadow. TRE it was worth £10; and afterwards £6; now £12.

• Ralph holds of the bishop TADWORTH. 2 brothers held it of King Edward, and they could go where they would. It was then assessed at 5 hides; now at 1½ hides. There is land for 2 ploughs. In demesne [are] 1½ [ploughs]; and 3 villans and 4 bordars with 1½ ploughs. There is 1 slave, and 1 pig from the woodland. TRE it was worth 40*s*.; and afterwards, as now, 30*s*.

• Richard holds of the bishop FETCHAM. Bicga held it of King Edward. It was then assessed at 8½ hides; now at 4 hides. There is land for 5 ploughs. In demesne is 1 [plough];

and 8 villans and 3 bordars with 1 plough. There are 2 slaves, and the sixth part of a mill, and the third part of another mill, and 10 acres of meadow; and from the pannage and herbage, 13 pigs. From the mills, 6½*s*. TRE, as now, worth 60*s*.; when received, 50*s*.

• Nigel holds of the bishop MICKLEHAM. Ansfrid held it of King Edward. Then, as now, it was assessed at 5 hides. There is land for 4 ploughs. In demesne are 2 ploughs, and 4 villans and 4 bordars and 2 slaves. There is a church, and 2 acres of meadow, [and] woodland for 3 pigs. TRE it was worth £3; and afterwards 50*s*.; now £4.

• Hugh de Port holds of the bishop GREAT BURGH. 3 free men held it, and they could go where they would. It was then assessed at 5 hides; now at 2½ hides. Hugh holds these 4 manors as 1 manor. It is valued in Wallington Hundred.

IN 'ELMBRIDGE' HUNDRED

• The same Hugh holds of the bishop 1 free hide in Esher, and a certain woman [holds] of him. There is 1 villan. It is worth 5*s*. When Hugh was seised of this land, he did not have the livery officer or the king's writ for it, as the hundred testifies.

• Herfrid holds of the bishop WEYBRIDGE. 2 sisters held it TRE, and they could turn with the land where they would. It was then assessed at 4 hides; now at 2 hides. There is 1 villan and 1 bordar, and 16 acres of meadow, [and] woodland for 5 pigs. It is and was worth 40*s*. When the bishop was seised of this land, they did not have the livery officer or the king's writ for it, as the hundred testifies.

IN KINGSTON HUNDRED

• Wadard holds of the bishop THAMES DITTON. Leofgar held it of Harold, and served him, but could have gone with the land where he would. When he died, he divided this land between his 3 sons, TRE. It was then assessed at 6 hides; now at 2½ hides. There is land for 2 ploughs. There are 1½ ploughs, and 4 bordars and 4 slaves, and part of a mill rendering 15*d*., and 4 acres of meadow, [and] woodland for 20 pigs. TRE it was worth £4; and afterwards 40*s*.; now £4. He who holds it of Wadard renders him 50*s*. and the service of 1 knight.

• The bishop himself has in SOUTHWARK 1 minster and 1 tideway. King Edward held them on the day on which he died. He who had the church held it of the king. From the dues of the waterway, where ships used to put in, the king had 2 parts, Earl Godwine the third. But the men of the hundred, both French and English, testify that the Bishop of Bayeux commenced a suit concerning these [tolls] with Ranulph the sheriff; but he, understanding that the suit was not being justly conducted to the king's advantage, withdrew the suit. The bishop at first gave the church and the tidal stream to Adelold, then to Ralph in exchange for a house. The sheriff also denies that he had ever received the king's precept or seal concerning this matter.

The men of Southwark testify that TRE no one took toll on the strand or on the water front except the king, and if anyone committing a trespass there had been charged, he paid a fine to the king. If, however, he had escaped uncharged to [the jurisdiction of] him who had sake and soke, that man was to have the fine from the accused.

The men of Southwark themselves have proved their right to an enclosure and its toll [belonging to] the farm of Kingston upon Thames. Count Eustace held this. What the king has in Southwark is valued at £16.

• In Wotton Hundred and in the manor of Sutton [in Shere] the Bishop of Bayeux has 2½ hides. Heoruwulf held them TRE, and could go where he would. They were then assessed at 2½ hides; now at nothing. These are enumerated and valued in the bishop's manor of Bramley.

VI. THE LAND OF THE CHURCH OF WESTMINSTER

IN BRIXTON HUNDRED

• ST PETER of Westminster holds BATTERSEA. Earl Harold held it. It was then assessed at 72 hides, and now at 18 hides. There is land [. . .]. In demesne are 3 ploughs; and 45 villans and 16 bordars with 14 ploughs. There are 8 slaves, and 7 mills rendering £42. 9*s*. 8*d*., or wheat of the same value, and 82 acres of meadow, and woodland for 50 pigs as pannage, and in Southwark 1 bordar paying 12*d*. From the toll of Wandsworth, £6. From a villan having 10 pigs, 1 pig; if less, he gives nothing.

A knight holds 4 hides of the land of this manor. His livestock is reckoned above with the other.

The whole was worth TRE £80; and afterwards £30; now £75. 9*s*. 8*d*. King William gave this manor to St Peter's in exchange for Windsor [Berks.].

• The Count of Mortain holds of the land of this manor 1½ hides, which belonged to it TRE, and for some time afterwards. Gilbert the priest holds 3 hides; they had been [held] in the same way. The Bishop of Lisieux [holds] 2 hides of which the church was seised in the time of King William; and afterwards the Bishop of Bayeux disseised it. The Abbot of Chertsey holds 1 hide, [. . .] which the reeve of this vill, on account of some enmity, took away from this manor, and put in Chertsey. ☒

IN WALLINGTON HUNDRED

• The Abbey of Westminster itself holds MORDEN. TRE it was assessed at 12 hides; now at 3 hides. There is land [. . .]. In demesne are 3 ploughs; and 8 villans and 5 cottars with 4 ploughs. There is 1 slave, and a mill rendering 40*s*. TRE it was worth £6; now £10, and yet it renders £15.

IN KINGSTON HUNDRED

• The abbey itself holds CLAYGATE. TRE it was assessed at 2½ hides; now at half a hide. There is land for 2 ploughs. In demesne is 1 [plough]; and 3 villans and 2 bordars with 1 plough. There are 5 acres of meadow, [and] woodland for 1 pig. TRE it was worth 40*s*.; now 50*s*.

IN BRIXTON HUNDRED

• The abbey itself holds UPPER TOOTING. Swein held it of King Edward, and it was assessed at 4 hides. There is land for 1½ ploughs. There are 2 villans with half a plough, and 3 acres of meadow. TRE, as now, worth 40*s*.; when received, 20*s*. Earl Waltheof received this land of Swein after the death of King Edward, and pledged it for 2 marks of gold to Alnoth of London, who granted it to St Peter's for his soul: namely, what he had there. Odbert holds it of St Peter's, and has paid nothing for geld.

IN 'GODLEY' HUNDRED

• The abbey itself holds PYRFORD. Harold held it of King Edward. Before Harold had it, it was assessed at 27 hides; after he had it, at 16 hides at Harold's pleasure. The men of the hundred have never heard nor seen the writ on the king's behalf, which had fixed it at so much. [There is] land for 13 ploughs. Now it pays geld for 8 hides.

In demesne is 1 plough; and 37 villans and 14 bordars with 6 ploughs. There are 3 slaves, and 2 mills rendering 10*s*., and 15 acres of meadow. From the pannage and herbage, 80 pigs. TRE it was worth £12; and afterwards £10; now £18. The king has 3 hides of this land in his forest.

VII. THE LAND OF ST PETER OF WINCHESTER

IN WALLINGTON HUNDRED

• The ABBEY OF ST PETER of Winchester holds SANDERSTEAD. TRE it was assessed at 18 hides; now at 5 hides. There is land for 10 ploughs. In demesne is 1 [plough]; and 21 villans and 1 cottar with 8 ploughs.

There are 4 slaves, [and] woodland for 30 pigs. TRE it was worth 100*s*.; and afterwards £7; now £12, yet it renders £15.

VIII. THE LAND OF THE CHURCH OF CHERTSEY

IN WALLINGTON HUNDRED

• THE ABBEY OF ST PETER of CHERTSEY holds 'WADDINGTON' [in Coulsdon]. TRE it was assessed at 20 hides; now at 5 hides. There is land for 8 ploughs. In demesne is 1 plough; and 17 villans and 2 cottars with 5 ploughs. There is a church, [and] woodland for 6 pigs as pannage. TRE it was worth £6; now £7.

[7] • The abbey itself holds COULSDON. TRE it was assessed at 20 hides; now at 3½ hides. There is land for 10 ploughs. In demesne is 1 plough; and 10 villans and 4 cottars with 6 ploughs. There is a church, [and] woodland for 3 pigs. TRE it was worth £6; now £7.

[7] • The abbey itself holds SUTTON [near Cheam]. TRE it was assessed at 30 hides; now at 8½ hides. There is land for 15 ploughs. In demesne are 2 ploughs; and 21 villans and 4 cottars with 13 ploughs. There are 2 churches, and 2 slaves, and 2 acres of meadow, [and] woodland for 10 pigs. TRE it was worth £20; now £15.

IN TANDRIDGE HUNDRED

• The abbey itself holds 2 hides of land, and William holds of the abbot. But the men testify that it was the demesne land of Alwine TRE, and he could go where he would. [. . .] It was then assessed at 2 hides; now at nothing. There is 1 bordar and 1 slave. TRE it was worth 20*s*.; and afterwards 5*s*.; now 10*s*.

IN 'ELMBRIDGE' HUNDRED

[7] • The abbey itself holds COBHAM. TRE it was assessed at 30 hides; now at 12½ hides. There is land for 10 ploughs. In demesne is 1 plough; and 29 villans and 6 cottars with 9 ploughs. There are 3 mills rendering 13*s*. 4*d*., and 1 acre of meadow, [and] woodland for 40 pigs. TRE it was worth £20; now £14.

• William de Watteville holds 2 hides of the abbey itself. An Englishman held them TRE, and in the lifetime of this king he gave this land to the same church in alms. This land belongs to the manor of Esher. There are 6 villans with 2 ploughs. TRE, as now, worth 14*s*. 6*d*.

In the same vill of Esher the same William has of the Abbey of Chertsey, as he says, 3½ hides. TRE 1 man and 2 women held them, and they could turn where they would; but for security they placed themselves with the land under the abbey. There are 2 villans with 1 plough. TRE it was worth 16*s*.; and afterwards 5*s*.; now 10*s*. These aforesaid 5½ hides are assessed at 5 virgates.

IN 'COPTHORNE' HUNDRED

[7] • The abbey itself holds EPSOM. TRE it was assessed at 34 hides; now at 11 hides. There is land for 17 ploughs. In demesne is 1 [plough]; and 34 villans and 4 bordars with 17 ploughs. There are 2 churches, and 6 slaves, and 2 mills rendering 10*s*., and 24 acres of meadow, [and] woodland for 20 pigs. TRE it was worth £20; now £17.

• In WEYBRIDGE the abbey itself hitherto has held [. . .] 2 hides. Alfred held them TRE and after his [the king's] death, and could turn where he would. Then, as now, [there were] 2 hides. There are 3 villans, and 8 acres of meadow, [and] woodland for 2 pigs. [It has] always [been worth] 20*s*.

In the same vill an Englishman has 2 hides of the abbey itself. He himself held them TRE, and could turn with them where he would. There is 1 plough, and 2 villans with half a plough, and 8 acres of meadow, [and] woodland for 2 pigs. It is and was worth 20*s*.

IN KINGSTON HUNDRED

• Eadric holds of the abbey itself half a hide which the abbey held for 2 years before the death of King Edward. 3 men held it of the king himself previously, but they could not withdraw without the king's precept, because they were beadles in Kingston upon Thames. Then, as now, it was assessed at half a hide. There is land for 3 oxen. There are 7 oxen, with 1 bordar, and 2 acres of meadow. TRE it was worth 7*s*.; now 8*s*.

[X] • William de Watteville holds OLD MALDEN of the fief of the abbot. The abbot held it TRE. It was then assessed at 2 hides; now at 1 hide less 1 virgate. There is land for 1 plough. There are 4 villans with half a plough. It is and was worth 20*s*.

[7] • The abbey itself holds in demesne PETERSHAM. TRE it was assessed at 10 hides; now at 4 hides. There is land for 5 ploughs. In
[X] demesne is 1 plough; and 15 villans and 2 bordars with 4 ploughs. There is a church, and a fishery rendering 1,000 eels and 1,000 lampreys, and 3 acres of meadow. TRE it was worth 100*s*.; now £6. 10*s*.

• Hamo the sheriff holds [?]STREATHAM of the abbey itself. Wulfweard held it of King Edward, and could go where he would. It was then assessed at 1 hide. There is land for 1 plough. There are 2 bordars. It is and was worth 20*s*.

IN 'ELMBRIDGE' HUNDRED

In this hundred the abbey itself holds 3 virgates of land

• Reginald holds 1 hide in Esher of the abbey itself, and has paid geld for 15 acres. A certain woman held it TRE, and could go where she would, but for security she put herself under the abbey. There are 3 villans. It is worth 7*s*.

IN EFFINGHAM HUNDRED

[7] • The abbey itself holds GREAT BOOKHAM. TRE it was
[2] assessed at 26 hides; and now at 13 hides. There is land for 19 ploughs. In demesne is 1 plough; and 32 villans and 4 bordars with 18 ploughs. There is a church, and 3 slaves, and a mill rendering 10*s*., and 6 acres of meadow. [There is] woodland for 80 pigs. From the herbage, 30 pigs. Of this land, Gunfrid holds 1 hide, and he has there 1 plough. The whole manor TRE was worth £16; now £15.

• The abbey itself lies in 'GODLEY' HUNDRED, and the vill itself [Chertsey] TRE, as now, was assessed at 5 hides. There is land [. . .]. In demesne are 2 ploughs; and 39 villans and 20 bordars with 17 ploughs. There is a mill at the hall, and 200 acres of meadow. [There is] woodland for 50 pigs as pannage, and a forge which serves the hall. Of these 5 hides, Richard Sturmy holds 2½ hides under King William. But the hundred testifies that his predecessor held of the abbey, nor could he go elsewhere without leave of the abbot. He has in demesne there 1 plough; and 1 villan and 4 bordars with 1 plough. The whole manor TRE was worth £18; now £22; what Richard holds [is worth] 40*s*.

[7] • The abbey itself holds THORPE. In 'Godley' HUNDRED. TRE it was assessed at 10 hides; now at 7 hides. There is land [. . .]. In demesne is 1 plough; and 24 villans and 12 bordars with 8 ploughs. There are 33 acres of meadow. From the herbage, 24 pigs. TRE, as now, worth £12.

IN EFFINGHAM HUNDRED

• Osweald holds of the church itself EFFINGHAM. He himself held it TRE. It was then assessed at 6 hides; now at 2½ hides. There is land for 2 ploughs. There are 2 villans and 9 bordars with half a plough, and 1 acre of meadow, and from the woodland, 10 pigs as pannage. It is and was worth 40*s*.

IN 'GODLEY' HUNDRED

[7] • The abbey itself holds EGHAM. TRE it was assessed at 40 hides; now at 15 hides. There is land for 40 ploughs. In demesne are 2 ploughs; and 25 villans and 32 bordars with 10 ploughs. There are 120 acres of meadow. [There is] woodland for 50 pigs as pannage. From the herbage, 25 pigs. TRE it was worth £40; now £30. 10*s*. Of this land Joscelin holds 3 hides, which were of the abbey's demesne TRE.

[7] • The abbey itself holds CHOBHAM. TRE, as now, it was assessed at 10 hides. There is land for 12 ploughs. In demesne is 1 [plough]; and 29 villans and 6 bordars with 11 ploughs. There
[2] are 3 slaves, and 10 acres of meadow, [and] woodland for 130 pigs. Of this land, Odin holds of the abbot 4 hides, [and] Corbelin 2 hides of the land of the villans. In demesne [is] 1 plough; and 7 villans and 4 bordars with 3 ploughs. There is a church and another chapel. [continued on f.34]

• In Wallington Hundred. Hamo the sheriff holds 1½ hides in fief of the Abbot of Chertsey. Alweard held them TRE, and could turn where he would. In demesne is 1 plough, with 6 cottars and 3 slaves, and 11 acres of meadow. TRE and afterwards, as now, worth 20*s*.

• The same Hamo holds half a hide of the abbey itself. Wulfweard held it TRE, and could turn where he would. There is 1 cottar, and 5 acres of meadow. It is and was worth 5*s*. These 2 hides which Hamo holds were assessed at 2 hides TRE; now at half [a hide].

• In Brixton Hundred. The same Hamo holds Tooting [?Graveney] of the Abbot of Chertsey. It was assessed at 6 hides less 1 virgate TRE; now at nothing. There is land for 3 ploughs. In demesne is 1 plough; and 3 villans and 2 bordars with 1 plough. There is a church, and 4 acres of meadow. TRE it was worth 40*s*.; afterwards 20*s*.; now 70*s*.

• The same Hamo holds in Tooting [?Graveney] 1 hide of the Abbot of Chertsey. Osweard held it of King Edward, and could go where he would. There is 1 villan with half a plough, and 1 acre of meadow. TRE [it was worth] 15*s*.; now 10*s*.

• In Reigate Hundred. William de Watteville held Chipstead of the Abbot of Chertsey. Thorgisl and Ulf held it TRE. The land of Thorgisl belonged to the abbey. Ulf could go where he would. It was then assessed at 5 hides; now at 1 hide. There are 2 villans and 1 bordar. When William left, it was at farm for 40*s*.

[Blank in MS]

[continued from f.32v]
The whole manor TRE was worth £16; now the monks' part [is worth] £12. 10s., but the men's [part] 60s.

• Wulfwine holds of the abbey itself BYFLEET. The same man held it TRE. It was then assessed at 8 hides; now at $2\frac{1}{2}$ hides. There is land for 2 ploughs. In demesne is 1 plough; and 7 villans and 2 bordars with 2 ploughs. There is a church, and 3 slaves, and a mill rendering 5s. [There are] $1\frac{1}{2}$ fisheries rendering 325 eels, and 6 acres of meadow, [and] woodland for 10 pigs as pannage. TRE [it was worth] 100s.; now £4.

IN WOKING HUNDRED

7 • The abbey itself holds EAST CLANDON. TRE it was assessed at 10 hides; now at 4 hides. There is land for 5 ploughs. There are 6 villans and 12 bordars with 7 ploughs. [There is] woodland for 6 pigs. TRE it was worth £6; now £4, and yet the villans who hold it pay £6.

TRE the Abbot of Chertsey bought 2 hides in East Clandon, and put them in this manor. Eskil held them of the king. The Bishop of Bayeux put them in Bramley wrongfully, as the men of the hundred testify.

• The abbey itself holds HENLEY. Azur held it until he died, and gave it to the church for his soul in the time of King William, as the monks say, and they have the king's writ for it. TRE it was assessed at 8 hides; now at $5\frac{1}{2}$ hides. There is land for 5 ploughs. In demesne is 1 plough; and 10 villans and 6 bordars with 5 ploughs. There is a church, and 2 slaves, and 4 acres of meadow, [and] woodland for 50 pigs as pannage. TRE it was worth £6; now 100s.

IX. THE LAND OF SAINT-WANDRILLE

IN BRIXTON HUNDRED

• The Abbot of Saint-Wandrille holds WANDSWORTH, through Ingulf the monk. Swein held it of the king, and could go where he would. It was then assessed at 1 hide; now at nothing. There are 3 villans and 2 bordars with 1 plough. It was and is worth 20s.

X. THE LAND OF SAINT-LEUFROY

IN 'ELMBRIDGE' HUNDRED

• The Abbot of La-Croix-Saint-Leufroy holds 7 hides and 3 virgates of land in ESHER by gift of King William. Tovi held them of King Edward. [. . .] There is land for 2 ploughs. In demesne is 1 [plough]; and 4 villans and 11 cottars with 2 ploughs. It is worth £3. Since the SAINT had it, it has never paid geld.

XI. THE LAND OF THE CHURCH OF BATTLE

IN TANDRIDGE HUNDRED

• THE ABBOT of Battle holds LIMPSFIELD. Harold held it TRE. It was then assessed at 25 hides. Now, since the abbot received it, it is not assessed. There is land for 12 ploughs. In demesne are 5 ploughs; and 25 villans and 6 bordars with 14 ploughs. There is a mill rendering 2s., and a fishery, and 1 church, and 4 acres of meadow. [There is] woodland for 150 pigs as pannage, 2 stone quarries rendering 2s., and 3 nests of hawks in the wood, and 10 slaves. TRE it was worth £20; and afterwards £15; now £24. "BRAMESELLE" belonged to this manor TRE, as the men of the hundred say.

XII. THE LAND OF THE CHURCH OF BARKING

IN 'ELMBRIDGE' HUNDRED

• The Abbey of BARKING has 7 hides at WESTON GREEN. It is now assessed at 3 hides and 1 virgate. There is land for 3 ploughs. There are 9 villans with 3 ploughs. It is and was worth 40s. 7

IN WALLINGTON HUNDRED

• The abbey itself has 2 hides of land. TRE it was assessed at 2 hides; now at 1. There are 2 villans with half a plough, and 6 acres of meadow. TRE it was worth 1 mark of silver; now 20s.

XIII. THE LAND OF ST PAUL'S OF LONDON

IN BRIXTON HUNDRED

• The canons of ST PAUL'S of London hold BARNES. TRE it was assessed at 8 hides. These hides have paid, and do pay, geld with Mortlake, the archbishop's manor, and are accounted for there. There is land for 6 ploughs. In demesne are 2 ploughs; and 9 villans and 4 bordars with 3 ploughs, and 20 acres of meadow. TRE it was worth £6; now £7.

XIIII. THE LAND OF THE CHURCH OF LAMBETH

IN BRIXTON HUNDRED

• There is a manor [of] ST MARY'S which is called LAMBETH. Countess Gode, sister of King Edward, held it. It was then assessed at 10 hides; now at $2\frac{1}{2}$ hides. There is land for 12 ploughs. In demesne are 2 ploughs; and 12 villans and 27 bordars with 4 ploughs. There is a church, and 19 burgesses in London who pay 36s., and there are 3 slaves, and 16 acres of meadow, [and] woodland for 3 pigs. TRE, and afterwards, it was worth £10; now £11. Of this manor the Bishop of Bayeux has a piece of arable land, which before and after the death of Gode belonged to this church.

XV. THE LAND OF COUNT EUSTACE

IN TANDRIDGE HUNDRED

• Count EUSTACE holds OXTED. Gytha, the mother of Harold, held it TRE. It was then assessed at 20 hides; now at 5 hides There is land for 20 ploughs. In demesne are 2 ploughs; and 34 villans with 18 ploughs. There are 2 mills rendering 12s. 6d., and 4 acres of meadow. [There is] woodland for 100 pigs as pannage, and in Southwark 1 messuage rendering 2d., and 6 slaves and 9 bordars. There is a church. TRE it was worth £16; when received, £10; now £14.

• The count himself holds 'WALKINGSTEAD' [in Godstone]. Osweard held it of King Edward. It was then assessed at 40 hides; now at 6 hides. There is land for 30 ploughs. In demesne are 3 ploughs; and 39 villans and 2 bordars with 22 ploughs. There are 10 slaves, and a mill rendering 6s., and 3 acres of meadow, [and] woodland for 100 pigs. To this manor belong 15 messuages in Southwark and in London, rendering 6s. and 2,000 herrings. TRE it was worth £20; and afterwards £16; now £20, yet it renders £28 by weight.

IN REIGATE HUNDRED

• XVI. The Countess of Boulogne holds of the king NUTFIELD [Nutfield and South Nutfield]. Wulfwig held it of King Edward. It was then assessed at $13\frac{1}{2}$ hides; now at 3 hides. There is land for 12 ploughs. In demesne are 3 ploughs; and 25 villans and 10 bordars with 13 ploughs. There is a church, and 10 slaves, and a mill rendering 2s., and 10 acres of meadow. From the herbage, 12 pigs. TRE it was worth £13; and afterwards £10; now £15 at 20 [d.] to the ora.

XVII. THE LAND OF THE COUNT OF MORTAIN

IN BRIXTON HUNDRED

• The Count of MORTAIN holds LAMBETH. The canons of Waltham held it of Harold. It was then assessed at $6\frac{1}{2}$ hides; now at nothing. There is land for 6 ploughs. In demesne is 1 plough; and 5 villans and 12 bordars with 3 ploughs. There is 1 slave, and 6 acres of meadow. TRE it was worth 100s.; and afterwards, as now, £4.

• The same count has in Bermondsey 1 hide of the king's land, where his house is situated. There is 1 bordar. It is worth 8s.

IN WALLINGTON HUNDRED

• The same count has 2 hides of land and 1 virgate of the king. Æthelmær held them of King Edward. They are not now assessed. There are 4 villans and 9 cottars with 3 ploughs, and 9 acres of meadow. TRE, as now, worth 40s.; when received, 20s. |It was assessed at 2 hides and 1 virgate.| |[partly in margin]|

• The count himself holds [?] STREATHAM. TRE it was assessed at 5 hides; now at nothing. Harold held $1\frac{1}{2}$ hides; the canons of Waltham $1\frac{1}{2}$ hides. 3 sokemen held 2 hides, and could go where they would with them. There is land for 2 ploughs. There are 3 villans and 3 bordars with $2\frac{1}{2}$ ploughs. TRE it was worth 30s.; and afterwards 15s.; now 43s.

XVIII. THE LAND OF EARL ROGER

IN WOTTON HUNDRED

• Earl ROGER has of the king 1 hide, which belongs to Compton [near Chichester, Sussex], his manor in Sussex. TRE he who held [this] Compton held this hide of the king. It was then assessed at 1 hide; now at nothing. There is in demesne 1 plough. TRE it was worth 20s.; and afterwards, as now, 15s.

• Turold holds of Earl Roger BURPHAM. Osmund held it of King Edward. It was then assessed at 4 hides; now at 3 hides. There is land for 5 ploughs. In demesne is 1 plough; and 7 villans and 2 bordars with $3\frac{1}{2}$ ploughs, and a mill rendering 15*s*., and 25 acres of meadow. [There is] woodland for |80| pigs as pannage. There are 4 slaves. Of these hides, Godric has 1 hide which is called Wyke, in which was the hall belonging to this manor TRE; and there is in demesne 1 plough; and 4 villans and 3 bordars with 1 plough and 1 slave. [There is] woodland for 3 pigs. The whole manor, TRE and afterwards, was worth £8; now the lord [has] £7; his men 20*s*.

|[partly in margin]|

• Turold holds of the earl WORPLESDON. Osmund held it of King Edward. It was then assessed at 8 hides; now at $6\frac{1}{2}$ hides. There is land for 7 ploughs. In demesne is 1 plough; and 13 villans and 3 bordars with 6 ploughs. There is a church, and 1 slave, and 8 acres of meadow. [There is] woodland for 60 pigs as pannage. Of this land 2 knights hold 2 hides and 1 virgate; and they have there in demesne 2 ploughs, and 3 villans and 2 bordars, and a mill rendering 30*d*. The whole, TRE and afterwards, was worth £10; now the same, £10 all together.

IN GODALMING HUNDRED

• Turold holds of the earl LOSELEY. Osmund held it of King Edward. It was then assessed at 3 hides; now at 2 hides. There is land for 2 ploughs. In demesne is 1 plough; and 7 villans and 1 cottar with 3 ploughs. There are 2 slaves, and 5 acres of meadow. TRE it was worth 40*s*.; and afterwards 20*s*.; now 60*s*.

XIX. THE LAND OF RICHARD, SON OF COUNT GILBERT

IN TANDRIDGE HUNDRED

• RICHARD of TONBRIDGE holds in demesne CHEVINGTON. Alnoth held it of King Edward. It was then assessed at 20 hides; now at 6 hides. There is land for 12 ploughs. In demesne are $2\frac{1}{2}$ ploughs; and 23 villans and 1 bordar with 9 ploughs. There are 9 slaves, and a mill rendering 32*d*. From the herbage, 12 pigs. [There is] woodland for 50 pigs as pannage, and 16 acres of meadow. Of these hides, Roger holds half a hide, and he has there in demesne 1 plough, with 5 bordars. In Southwark [he has] 3 closes rendering 15*d*., and in London 2 messuages rendering 10*d*. TRE it was worth £11; and afterwards £6; now £10.

• Richard himself holds BLETCHINGLEY. Ælfheah and Alwine and Alnoth held it of King Edward. It was then assessed at 10 hides; now at 3 hides. There is land for 16 ploughs. There were 3 manors; now it is in 1. In demesne are 3 ploughs; and 20 villans and 4 bordars with 9 ploughs. There are 7 slaves, and 14 acres of meadow. From the woodland, 40 pigs, and from the herbage, 18 pigs. In London and Southwark, 7 messuages rendering 5*s*. 4*d*. Of these 10 hides, Odin holds $2\frac{1}{2}$ hides, and Lemei 2 hides, and Peter $1\frac{1}{2}$ hides. In demesne [is] 1 plough; and 3 villans and 2 bordars with 1 plough, and 3 acres of meadow. The whole manor TRE was worth £13; and afterwards £8; now what Richard holds [is worth] £12, what his men [hold] 73*s*. 4*d*.

• Robert de Watteville holds of Richard CHELSHAM. Wulfweard held it of King Edward. It was then assessed at 10 hides; now at 2 hides. There is land for 4 ploughs. In demesne are 2 ploughs; and 6 villans and 11 bordars with 3 ploughs. There are 4 slaves. 1 pig as a customary due. TRE it was worth £6; and afterwards £3; now £8.

• The wife of Salie holds of Richard TANDRIDGE. Thorbiorn held it of King Edward. It was then assessed at 10 hides; now at 2 hides. There is land for 10 ploughs. In demesne are 3 ploughs; and 20 villans and 10 bordars with 11 ploughs. There is 1 mill rendering 50*d*., and 5 acres of meadow. [There is] woodland for 40 pigs as pannage. From the herbage, 11 pigs. TRE it was worth £6; and afterwards 40*s*.; now £11.

• This same wife of Salie holds of Richard TILLINGDOWN. Alnoth held it of King Edward. It was then assessed at 10 hides; now at $1\frac{1}{2}$ hides. There is land for 4 ploughs. In demesne are 2 ploughs; and 5 villans and 8 slaves with $2\frac{1}{2}$ ploughs. There is a church. [There is] woodland for 30 pigs as pannage. TRE it was worth £7; and afterwards £3; now £6, and yet it renders £7.

• Robert de Watteville holds of Richard a manor which Azur held of King Edward. It was then assessed at 14 hides; now at 2 hides. There is land for 4 ploughs. In demesne are 2 ploughs; and 11 villans and 7 bordars with 3 ploughs. [There is] woodland for 5 pigs as pannage. There is a church. TRE, as now, worth £8; when received, 100*s*.

• The same Robert holds of Richard CHELSHAM. Toki held it of King Edward. It was then assessed at 10 hides; now at 2 hides. There is land for 4 ploughs. In demesne are 2 [ploughs]; and 11 villans and 7 bordars with 4 ploughs. There is a church, and 3 slaves. TRE, as now, worth £7; when received, £4.

• The same Robert holds of Richard FARLEIGH. Tovi held it of King Edward. It was then assessed at 6 hides; now at half a hide. There is land for $2\frac{1}{2}$ ploughs. In demesne is 1 [plough]; and 4 villans and 1 bordar with 1 plough. There is 1 slave, and 1 ox. TRE, as now, worth 60*s*.; when received, 20*s*.

• John holds of Richard WOLDINGHAM. Wulfstan held it of King Edward. It was then assessed at 8 hides; now at 1. There is land [. . .]. In demesne are $1\frac{1}{2}$ ploughs; and 6 villans and 3 bordars with 3 ploughs. There are 3 slaves. TRE, as now, worth £4; when received, 20*s*.

IN BRIXTON HUNDRED

• SAINTE-MARIE of Bec holds TOOTING BEC by gift of Richard. Starcher held it of King Edward. It was then assessed at 11 hides; and now the same, at 1 hide [*sic*]. There is land for 4 ploughs. In demesne are 2 ploughs; and 5 villans and 4 bordars with 3 ploughs. There are 10 acres of meadow. TRE, as now, worth 100*s*.; when received, 20*s*.

• This same church holds of Richard STREATHAM. Hearding held it of King Edward. It was then assessed at 5 hides; and now the same, at 1 hide and 1 virgate of land [*sic*]. There is land for 3 ploughs. In demesne is 1 plough; and 4 villans and 5 bordars with 2 ploughs. There is a chapel rendering 8*s*. There are 4 acres of meadow. [There is] woodland for 10 pigs. From the herbage, 1 pig out of 10 pigs. TRE it was worth 50*s*.; and afterwards, as now, 60*s*.

IN REIGATE HUNDRED

• William, nephew of Bishop Walkelin, holds of Richard CHIPSTEAD. Wulfnoth held it of King Edward. It was then assessed at 15 hides; now at 2 hides. There is land for 7 ploughs. In demesne are 2 [ploughs]; and 8 villans and 5 bordars with 5 ploughs. There are 5 slaves, and a mill rendering 20*s*. [There is] woodland for 5 pigs; Richard has retained another wood for himself. TRE it was worth £7; and afterwards 100*s*.; now £6.

• Siward holds of Richard "ORDE". Osweald held it of King Edward. Then, as now, it was assessed at half a hide. There is 1 villan with half a plough. TRE it was worth 30*s*.; and afterwards 2*s*.; now 20*s*.

• John holds of Richard BUCKLAND. Alnoth held it of King Edward. It was then assessed at 5 hides; now at 2 hides. There is land [. . .]. In demesne are $1\frac{1}{2}$ ploughs; and 17 villans and 8 bordars with 10 ploughs. There is a church, and 10 slaves, and a mill rendering 6*s*. TRE, and afterwards, it was worth 100*s*.; now £8.

IN WALLINGTON HUNDRED

• Robert de Watteville holds of Richard BEDDINGTON. Azur held it of King Edward. It was then assessed at 25 hides; now at 3 hides. There is land for 6 ploughs. In demesne is 1 plough;

and 16 villans and 14 cottars with 5 ploughs. There is a church, and 5 slaves, and 2 mills rendering 40*s.*, and 24 acres of meadow, [and] woodland for 5 pigs. 15 messuages in London, which belong to this manor, render 12*s.* 3*d.* TRE, as now, worth £10; when received, £6.

• Richard himself holds in demesne WOODMANSTERNE. Azur held it of King Edward. Then, as now, it was assessed at 15 hides, but it has never paid geld. There is land for 3 ploughs. In demesne are 2 ploughs; and 1 villan and 12 cottars with 3 ploughs. There are 18 slaves, and a church, and a mill rendering 20*s.*, and 4 acres of meadow, [and] woodland for 10 pigs. TRE it was worth £10; and afterwards 100*s.*; now £8.

IN 'COPTHORNE' HUNDRED

• John holds of Richard WALTON ON THE HILL. Alwine and Leofhelm and Coleman held it of King Edward as 3 manors, and could go where they would. It was then assessed at 15 hides; now at 2 hides and half a virgate. There is land for 5 ploughs. In demesne are 2½ ploughs; and 10 villans and 1 bordar with 2 ploughs, and 7 slaves. Of these hides, Roger holds 2 hides, and he has 1 plough there; and 1 messuage in Southwark. The whole TRE was worth £6; and afterwards £6; now £6.

IN 'ELMBRIDGE' HUNDRED

• Richard himself holds of the king 1 hide, which Almær held of King Edward, and he could go with it where he would. It has never paid geld since Richard has had it. It is worth 6*s.* 9*d.*

IN 'COPTHORNE' HUNDRED

• Osweald holds of Richard MICKLEHAM. The same man held it of King Edward. It was then assessed at 5 hides; now at 2 hides. There is land for 5 ploughs. In demesne is 1 plough; and 8 villans and 6 bordars with 4 ploughs. There are 2 slaves, and 1 acre of meadow, and 1 pig as pannage from the woodland. TRE it was worth 100*s.*; now £6.

IN KINGSTON HUNDRED

• Picot holds of Richard TOLWORTH. Alwine held it of King Edward, and he could go where he would. It was then assessed at 5 hides. [. . .] There is land for 3 ploughs. In demesne are 2 ploughs; and 7 villans and 8 bordars with 3 ploughs. There are 7 slaves, and a mill without rent, and 5½ acres of meadow, and half a virgate. TRE, as now, worth 60*s.*; when received, 20*s.*

• Picot holds of Richard LONG DITTON. Almær held it of King Edward. It was then assessed at 5 hides. This land, and that above, are now assessed at 4 hides. There is land for 4 ploughs. In demesne is 1 plough; and 2 villans and 9 bordars with 2½ ploughs. There is a church, and a mill rendering 9*s.*, [and] woodland for 15 pigs. There is 1 slave; and in Southwark 1 messuage rendering 500 herrings. TRE it was worth 60*s.*; and afterwards 30*s.*; now 50*s.*, yet it is at farm for £4.

• Picot holds of Richard a [piece of] land which is called 'EMBER' [in Thames Ditton]. Edwin and another man held it TRE, and they could go where they would. It was then assessed at half a hide; now at nothing. There are 6 oxen ploughing, with 2 bordars. It has always been worth 5*s.*

• Robert de Watteville holds of Richard OLD MALDEN. Hearding held it of King Edward. It was then assessed at 8 hides; now at 4. There is land for 5 ploughs. In demesne is 1 plough; and 14 villans and 2 bordars with 4 ploughs. There is a chapel, and 3 slaves, and a mill rendering 12*s.*, and 4 acres of meadow. From the herbage, 1 pig out of 7 pigs.

Of these hides, a knight holds 1 hide and 1 virgate, and there he has 1 plough, and 1 villan and 1 bordar, and 1 acre of meadow. The whole TRE was worth £7; and afterwards 100*s.*; now £6. 12*s.*

• The same Robert holds of Richard CHESSINGTON. Hearding held it of King Edward. It was then assessed at 5 hides; now at half a hide. There is land for 2 ploughs. There are 3 villans and 1 bordar with 1 plough, and half a mill rendering 2*s.* [There is] woodland for 30 pigs. TRE it was worth £4; and afterwards 40*s.*; now 70*s.*

A hide in OLD MALDEN which Robert de Watteville holds remains in dispute; and the men of the hundred say that Edward of Salisbury and Robert d'Oilly have proved their right to it against Richard of Tonbridge; and it has remained quit in the king's hands.

IN 'ELMBRIDGE' HUNDRED

• Richard himself holds WALTON-ON-THAMES. Hearding held it of King Edward. It was then assessed at 6 hides; now at 3 hides. There is land for 8 ploughs. In demesne are 2 ploughs; and 8 villans and 3 cottars with 3 ploughs. There is a church, and a mill rendering 12*s.* 6*d.*, and a fishery rendering 5*s.* TRE it was worth £8; and afterwards 100*s.*; now £14.

• The same Richard has in the manor of APPS 6 hides, which Abbot Wulfweald delivered to him in compensation for Walton-on-Thames, as Richard's men say. But the men of the hundred say that they have never seen the king's writ or livery officer who had given him seisin of it. 9 thegns held this land, and they could turn with it where they would. There are 10 villans and 6 cottars with 4 cottars [*sic*]. There are 2 slaves, and 46 acres of meadow, [and] woodland for 6 pigs. TRE it was worth £3; and afterwards 40*s.*; now £4.

• In Apps 1 villan holds half a hide, for which up till now he has given Richard's men 30*d.* for rent. Now it remains quit in the king's hands. And Picot holds of Richard in Apps half a hide which Almær held without gift of the king; now Picot holds it because his predecessor Almær held it. It is now worth 5*s.* Moreover, Picot holds of Richard in Apps half a hide which Almær held TRE, and could go with it where he would. Now it is worth 12*s.*

• John holds of Richard [East or West] MOLESEY. Ælfric held it of King Edward. It was then assessed at 3½ hides; and now at 5 virgates. There is land for 3 ploughs. In demesne is 1 plough; and 7 villans and 8 bordars with 2½ ploughs. There are 16 acres of meadow, [and] woodland for 4 pigs. TRE, as now, it was worth 60*s.*; when received, 40*s.*

In that manor John holds of Richard 1 hide, which was given in compensation for Walton-on-Thames. Wulfweard held it of King Edward. There are 2 villans with 2 oxen. It is and was worth 5*s.*

• Roger d'Abernon holds of Richard [East or West] MOLESEY. Toki held it of King Edward. It was then assessed at 6½ hides; now at 6 virgates. There is land for 3 ploughs. In demesne is 1 plough; and 4 villans and 4 cottars with 2½ ploughs. There are 6 slaves, and 16 acres of meadow, and woodland for 6 pigs. TRE it was worth £3; and afterwards 40*s.*; now 70*s.*

• Richard himself holds STOKE D'ABERNON. Beorhtsige Cild held it of King Edward. It was then assessed at 15 hides; now at 2 hides and 5 acres. There is land for 6 ploughs. In demesne are 2 ploughs; and 10 villans and 9 cottars with 2 ploughs. There is a church, and 7 slaves, and a mill rendering 7*s.*, and 4 acres of meadow, [and] woodland for 40 pigs. TRE, as now, worth £4; when received, £3.

• In the same manor the same Richard has 5 hides. Odo held them of King Edward. Now it is assessed at half a hide. There are 2 villans with 6 oxen, and a mill rendering 6*s.* There is land for 2 ploughs. It is and was worth 20*s.*

IN EFFINGHAM HUNDRED

• In 'DIRTHAM' [in Effingham] Richard holds 1½ hides. Almær held them of King Edward as a manor. The wife of Salie holds them of Richard, and she has there 1 villan and 2 bordars. It was worth 40*s.*; now 30*s.*

In the same 'DIRTHAM' [in Effingham] are 1½ hides which Ælfric held of King Edward as a manor, and he afterwards gave that land to his wife and daughter for the church of Chertsey, as the men of the hundred testify. Richard claims it. It does not belong to any manor, nor does he hold it as a manor, but it was delivered to him, and now 3 hides pay geld for 1½ hides. There is land for 2 ploughs. In this land of Ælfric there is in demesne 1 plough, and 2 bordars and 2 slaves. It is worth 40*s.*

IN BLACKHEATH HUNDRED

• Roger holds of Richard ALBURY. Azur held it of King Edward. It was then assessed at 4 hides; now at 2½ hides. There is land for 6 ploughs. In demesne is 1 [plough]; and 11 villans and 5 bordars with 6 ploughs. There is a church, and 4 slaves, and a mill rendering 5*s.*, [and] woodland for 30 pigs.

Of these hides, a knight holds 1 hide; and [has] there in demesne 1½ ploughs, and 1 villan and 1 slave; and an acre of meadow. The whole TRE was worth £10; and afterwards 100*s.*; now £9.

• Robert holds of Richard SHALFORD. 2 brothers held it TRE. Each one had his own house, and yet they resided in 1 court, and could go where they would. Then, as now, it was assessed at 4 hides. There is land for 6 ploughs. In demesne are 2 ploughs; and 29 villans and 11 bordars with 9 ploughs. There is a church, and 10 slaves, and 3 mills rendering 16*s.*, and 4 acres of meadow, [and] woodland for 20 pigs. Of these hides, a knight holds a virgate, where he has half a plough, and 1 slave and 5 bordars [. . .]. The whole TRE was worth £16; and afterwards £9; now £20. To this manor belongs a close in Guildford rendering 3*s.*

IN KINGSTON HUNDRED

• Ralph holds of Richard TOLWORTH. Eadmær held it, and could go where he would, TRE. It was then assessed at 5 hides; now at 2½ hides. There is land for 4 ploughs. In demesne is 1 plough; and 6 villans and 1 bordar with 2 ploughs. There are 2 slaves, and 5 acres of meadow. TRE, and afterwards, it was worth 40*s.*; now 60*s.*

IN 'COPTHORNE' HUNDRED

• Richard himself holds in demesne THORNCROFT. Cola held it of King Edward. There are now in demesne 2 ploughs; and 5 villans and 4 bordars with 2 ploughs. There are 9 slaves, and a mill rendering 20*s.*, and 5 acres of meadow, [and] woodland for 1 pig.

With that manor these lands were made over to Richard: 'West Betchworth' [in Dorking] at 6 hides; 1 hide and 1 virgate which Merewine held; and 1 hide which Alric and Almær held as a manor; and another hide which Coleman the huntsman held as a manor. These men were so free that they could go where they would; and these lands together with Thorncroft were assessed TRE at 25½ hides less 1 virgate; now at 4 hides less 4 acres. In the hide which Alric and Almær held is half a plough and 2 oxen in demesne. In Merewine's hide is 1 plough in demesne, and 3 acres of meadow. In Coleman's hide are 2 bordars. All together there is land for 5 ploughs. TRE Thorncroft was worth 100*s.*; when received, 60*s.*; now 110*s.* 2 hides [have] always [been worth] 30*s.*; Coleman's hide 10*s.*

In this hundred the Abbot of Westminster holds 2 hides, but they are valued in another hundred.

• In MICKLEHAM there belongs 1 hide which Sæmann held of King Edward, and now holds of King William. He has there in demesne 1 plough, and 3 bordars; and half an acre of meadow. It is and was worth 20*s.*

In the same place Godwine holds 1 virgate of King William. The same man held it of King Edward. It is worth 30*d.* a year.

In the same HUNDRED, William fitzAnsculf holds 2 hides, but they are valued in another hundred.

⊠

IN EFFINGHAM HUNDRED

• Osweald holds of Richard EFFINGHAM. Azur held it of King Edward. It was then assessed at 6 hides; now at 2½ hides. With these 6 hides Osweald holds 1 hide and 1 virgate of land which a free man held under King Edward, but for a certain need of his he sold it to Azur in the time of King William. There is land for 5 ploughs all together. In demesne are 2 ploughs; and 6 villans and 5 bordars with 2 ploughs. There are 6 slaves, and 4 acres of meadow, and woodland for 5 pigs. From the herbage, 3 pigs. TRE it was worth 100*s.*; and afterwards £4. 10*s.*; now £6.

IN WOKING HUNDRED

• Richard himself holds OCKHAM in demesne. Almær held it of King Edward. It was then assessed at 9 hides; now at 1½ hides. There is land for 4 ploughs. In demesne is 1 plough; and 6 villans and 2 bordars with 2 ploughs. There is a church, and 3 slaves, and 2 fisheries rendering 10*d.*, and 2 acres of meadow. [There is] woodland for 60 pigs. It is and always was worth 100*s.*

• Ralph holds of Richard OCKLEY. Almær held it of King Edward. Then, as now, it was assessed at 1 hide. There is land for 4 ploughs. In demesne is 1 [plough]; and 9 villans and 3 bordars with 4 ploughs. [There is] woodland for 20 pigs, and 2 slaves. TRE it was worth 70*s.*; and afterwards, as now, the same.

In this manor Richard himself holds half a hide. Alwine held it TRE, and could go with it where he would. Then [it was assessed] at half a hide; now at nothing. It is valued in Ockley.

IN WOTTON HUNDRED

• Richard himself holds in demesne 'WEST BETCHWORTH' [in Dorking]. Cola held it of King Edward. It was then assessed at 6 hides; and now at 2 hides. There is land for 7 ploughs. In demesne is 1 plough; and 6 villans and 10 bordars with 3 ploughs. There are 6 slaves, and a mill rendering 10*s.*, and 3 acres of meadow. [There is] woodland for 80 pigs. From the herbage, 6 pigs. There is a church. TRE, and afterwards, [worth] £9; now £8.

• Richard himself holds HARTSHURST. Almær held it of King Edward. Then, as now, it was assessed at 2 hides. There is land for 4 ploughs. There are 8 villans with 3 ploughs. [There is] woodland for 15 pigs. TRE and afterwards, as now, worth 45*s.* This land belonged to a certain free man, and he could go with it where he pleased; nor does it belong to any manor of Richard.

XX. THE LAND OF WILLIAM DE BRAOSE

IN 'COPTHORNE' HUNDRED

• William de Braose holds TADWORTH, and Halsart [holds] of him. Godtovi held it of Earl Harold, and could go where he would. It was then assessed at 5 hides; now at half a hide. There is land for 3 ploughs. In demesne is 1 plough; and 2 villans and 5 bordars with 1 plough. [There is] woodland for 3 pigs. TRE it was worth 100*s.*; and afterwards 20[*s.*]; now 45[*s.*].

IN EFFINGHAM HUNDRED

• Halsart holds of William LITTLE BOOKHAM. Godtovi held it of Earl Harold. It was then assessed at 5 hides; now at 2 hides. There is land for 3 ploughs. In demesne is 1 [plough]; and 3 villans and 4 bordars with 1 plough. There are 4 acres of meadow. From the pannage and herbage, 11 pigs. TRE, and afterwards, it was worth 50*s.*; now 60*s.*

XXI. THE LAND OF WILLIAM FITZANSCULF

IN WALLINGTON HUNDRED

• WILLIAM fitzAnsculf holds 'WHITFORD' [in Mitcham], and William the chamberlain [holds] of him. Lang held held [*sic*] it of King Edward. It was then assessed at 2 hides; now at 1 hide. There is land [. . .]. In demesne is 1 plough; and 2 villans with 1 plough, and a mill rendering 20*s.*, and 24 acres of meadow. TRE it was
⊠ worth 50*s.*; and afterwards 22*s.*; now 60*s.*

• The same William holds MITCHAM. Lemar held it of King Edward. Then, as now, it was assessed at 2 hides and 1 virgate. There are 2 villans and 6 cottars, and half a mill rendering 20*s.* TRE, as now, worth 40*s.*; when received, 13*s.* 4*d.*

IN BRIXTON HUNDRED

• William himself holds WANDSWORTH. 6 sokemen held it of King Edward, and they could go where they would. There were 2 halls.

Then, as now, it was assessed at 12 hides. There is land for 4 ploughs. Ansculf had this land after he received the sheriffdom; but the men of the hundred say that they have not seen the [king's] seal nor livery officer.

Ansfrid['s land was assessed at] 5 hides; now at 1 hide. Ealdræd['s at] 3 hides; now at nothing. Wulfweard['s at] 3 hides. Walter the vineyard-keeper at 1 hide. They did not pay geld. In their land are 2½ ploughs in demesne; and 5 villans and 22 bordars with 2 ploughs, and 22 acres of meadow. The whole manor TRE was worth 110*s*.; and afterwards 50*s*.; now £8 all together.

IN WOTTON HUNDRED

● Baldwin holds MILTON of William himself. Wulfric held it of King Edward. It was then assessed at 6 hides; now at 4½ hides. There is land for 5 ploughs. In demesne is 1 plough; and 10 villans and 9 bordars with 4 ploughs, and 4 slaves, and a mill rendering 2*s*., and 2 acres of meadow. [There is] woodland for 9 pigs. From the herbage, 10 pigs. TRE it was worth 70*s*.; and afterwards, as now, 60*s*.

In the HUNDRED of 'Copthorne' are 2 hides which belong to this manor. They are worth 20*s*.

● The same Baldwin holds of William 1 hide at Anstie. Ordwig held it; and Baldwin holds half a hide at "Litelfeld". Ælfhere held it. These 2 could go with their lands where they would. There is 1 plough in demesne, with 1 bordar. It is worth 11*s*. 3*d*.

● William himself holds ABINGER. Huscarl held it of King Edward. It was then assessed at 6 hides; now at 4 hides. There is land for 9 ploughs. In demesne are 2 ploughs; and 10 villans and 7 bordars with 5 ploughs. There is a church, and 5 slaves, and a mill rendering 6*s*., and 3 acres of meadow. From the herbage and pannage, 40 pigs. TRE it was worth £8; and afterwards, as now, £7.

● William himself holds PADDINGTON. Huscarl held it of King Edward. It was then assessed at 4 hides; now at 3 hides. There is land for 9 ploughs. In demesne is nothing; but there are 12 villans and 5 bordars with 6 ploughs, and a mill rendering 6*s*., and 4 acres of meadow. [There is] woodland for 40 pigs. From the herbage, 15 pigs. Of this manor, Hugh, a man of William, holds 3 hides, with a hall, and 1 plough in demesne. The whole manor TRE was worth £9; and afterwards £7; now the same £7.

XXII. THE LAND OF WALTER FITZOTHER

IN GODALMING HUNDRED

● WALTER fitzOther holds COMPTON. Beorhtsige held it of King Edward. It was then assessed at 14 hides; now at 11 hides. There is land for 10 ploughs. In demesne are 3 ploughs; and 21 villans and 8 cottars with 6 ploughs. There are 7 slaves, and 7 acres of meadow. There is a church. TRE it was worth £8; and afterwards £6; now £9.

● Tezelin holds of Walter HURTMORE. Alwine held it of King Edward. It was then assessed at 15 hides; now at 3 hides. There is land for 3 ploughs. In demesne are 2 ploughs; and 3 villans and 2 cottars with 1½ ploughs. There is 1 mill rendering 11*s*., and 6 acres of meadow. TRE it was worth 50*s*.; afterwards 30*s*.; now 100*s*.

● Walter himself holds PEPER HAROW, and Gerard [holds] of him. Alweard held it of King Edward. It was then assessed at 5 hides; now at 3 hides. There is land for 3 ploughs. In demesne are 2 ploughs, and a mill rendering 15*s*., and 7 acres of meadow. There are 4 villans and 3 cottars with 1 plough. TRE, and afterwards, it was worth 30*s*.; now 100*s*.

IN KINGSTON HUNDRED

● Walter himself holds 1 man of the soke of Kingston upon Thames, to whom he has committed the charge of the king's wild mares, but we know not on what terms. This man holds 2 hides, but he has no right in the land itself. It was assessed at 2 hides; now at nothing. There is 1 plough in demesne, with 3 slaves, and 1 fishery rendering 125 eels, and 1 acre of meadow. It is and was always worth 30*s*. §1

XXIII. THE LAND OF WALTER DE DOUAI

IN WALLINGTON HUNDRED

● WALTER de Douai holds 2 hides of the king, as he says. But the men of the hundred say that they have never seen the writ or the king's commissioner who had given him seisin of it. But this they testify, that a certain free man holding this land, and able to go where he would, commended himself into Walter's hand for his own protection. This land is and was worth 20*s*.

XXIIII. THE LAND OF GILBERT FITZRICHER

● GILBERT fitzRicher de l'Aigle holds WITLEY. Earl Godwine held it. It was then assessed at 20 hides; now at 12 hides. There is land for 16 ploughs. In demesne are 2 ploughs; and 37 villans and 3 cottars with 13 ploughs. There is a church, and 3 acres of meadow, [and] woodland for 30 pigs. TRE, and afterwards, it was worth £15; now £16.

XXV. THE LAND OF GEOFFREY DE MANDEVILLE

IN BRIXTON HUNDRED

● GEOFFREY de Mandeville holds CLAPHAM. Thorbiorn held it of King Edward. It was then assessed at 10 hides; now at 3 hides. There is land for 7 ploughs. In demesne is 1 plough; and 8 villans and 3 bordars with 5 ploughs. There are 5 acres of meadow. TRE it was worth £10; afterwards the same; now £7. 10*s*. The men say that Geoffrey has this manor wrongfully, because it does not belong to Esger's land. What Geoffrey gave in alms from this manor is worth 20*s*.

XXVI.

● GEOFFREY Orlateile holds BALHAM without the gift of the king and without warrant. Eskil held it of Earl Harold. It was then assessed at 5 hides; now at nothing. There is land for 2 ploughs. In demesne is 1 [plough]; and 1 villan and 1 bordar with half a plough. There is 1 slave, and 8 acres of meadow. TRE it was worth £6; afterwards 20*s*.; now 40*s*.

IN WALLINGTON HUNDRED

● Geoffrey himself holds CARSHALTON. 5 free men [held it] of King Edward, and they could go where they would. Of these, 1 held 2 hides, and 4 [held] 6 hides apiece. There were 5 manors. Now it is in 1 manor. It was then assessed at 27 hides; now at 3½ hides. There is land for 10 ploughs. In demesne is 1 [plough]; and 9 villans and 9 cottars with 5 ploughs. There is a church, and 7 slaves, and 12 acres of meadow. The men of the shire and of the hundred say that they have never seen the writ or the livery officer who on the king's behalf had given Geoffrey seisin of this manor. TRE it was worth £20; when he was seised of it, 100*s*.; now £10. Of these hides, Wesman holds 6 hides of Geoffrey son of Count Eustace. Geoffrey de Mandeville gave him [i.e. Geoffrey] this land with his daughter. In demesne is 1 plough; and 3 villans and 1 cottar with 3 ploughs, and a mill rendering 35*s*., and 3 slaves, and 10 acres of meadow. [There is] woodland for 2 pigs. There is land for 2 ploughs. TRE it was worth £4; and afterwards 40*s*.; now 110*s*. Of the same hides, a certain smith of the king's has half a hide, which TRE he received with his wife, but he has never done service for it.

IN WOKING HUNDRED

● Geoffrey himself holds WANBOROUGH. It is not [part] of Esger's land. Swein and Leofwine, brothers, held it of King Edward. It was then assessed at 7 hides; now at 3 hides. There is land for 7 ploughs. There were 2 manors; now there is 1. In demesne is 1 plough; and 12 villans and 17 bordars with 8 ploughs. There is a church, and 8 slaves, and 6 acres of meadow, [and] woodland for 30 pigs. The whole TRE was worth £7; afterwards 100*s*.; now £7.

IN WOKING HUNDRED

§1 ● Walter fitzOther holds WEST HORSLEY. Beorhtsige held it of King Edward. It was then assessed at 10 hides; now at 8 hides. There is land for 6 ploughs. In demesne are 2 ploughs; and 14 villans and 5 bordars with 5 ploughs. There is a church, and 8 slaves, [and] woodland for 20 pigs. TRE it was worth £8; afterwards 100*s*.; now £6. Of this land, an Englishman holds 1 hide; and he has 1 plough there, with 1 bordar. It is worth 20*s*.

XXVII. THE LAND OF EDWARD OF SALISBURY

IN 'ELMBRIDGE' HUNDRED

● EDWARD of Salisbury holds WALTON-ON-THAMES. Azur held it of King Edward. It was then assessed at 6 hides; now at 3 hides. There is land for 8 ploughs. In demesne are 2 ploughs; and 8 villans and 3 cottars with 7 ploughs. There are 8 slaves, and a mill rendering 12*s*. 6*d*., and 40 acres of meadow, [and] woodland for 50 pigs. There is a forester, paying 10*s*. TRE it was worth £8; afterwards 100*s*.; now £12, yet it renders £14.

IN GODALMING HUNDRED

● Ranulph holds of Edward HAMBLEDON. Azur held it of King Edward. It was then assessed at 5 hides; now at 3 hides. There is land for 4 ploughs. In demesne are 2 ploughs; and 8 villans and 1 cottar with 5 ploughs. There are 13 slaves, and a mill rendering 30*d*., and 3 acres of meadow, [and] woodland for 30 pigs. It is and always was worth 100*s*.

IN WOKING HUNDRED

● Hugh holds of Edward WEST CLANDON. Fulcwig held it TRE. It was then assessed §2

§2 at 5 hides; now at 2½ hides. There is land for 3 ploughs. In demesne is 1 [plough]; and 2 villans and 5 bordars with 1½ ploughs. [There is] a mill rendering 3*s*. There is a church, and woodland for 5 pigs. It was worth 50*s*.; now 60*s*.

XXVIII. THE LAND OF ROBERT MALET

IN WOKING HUNDRED

● ROBERT Malet holds SUTTON [in Woking]. Wynsige held it of King Edward. It was then assessed at 5 hides; now at 3 hides. There is land for 3 ploughs. In demesne is 1 [plough]; and 5 villans and 5 bordars with 2 ploughs. There are 6 slaves, and a mill rendering 5*s.*, and 20 acres of meadow, [and] woodland for 25 pigs. TRE, and afterwards, it was worth £8; now 100*s.* Durand was seised of this land, and the men say that he has it wrongfully, for none of them has seen the king's writ or livery officer.

XXIX. THE LAND OF MILES CRISPIN

IN WALLINGTON HUNDRED

● MILES Crispin holds BEDDINGTON, and William fitzTurold [holds] of him. Ulf held it of King Edward. It was then assessed at 25 hides; now at 3 hides. There is land for 6 ploughs. In demesne is 1 plough; and 13 villans and 13 cottars with 6 ploughs. There is 1 slave, and 2 mills rendering 35*s.*, and 20 acres of meadow, [and] woodland for 5 pigs. TRE it was worth £10; afterwards £6; now £9. 10*s.* From this manor [. . .] have been taken 21 messuages which Earl Roger holds, 13 in London, 8 in Southwark. They render 12*s.*

IN KINGSTON HUNDRED

● Miles himself holds CHESSINGTON. Magni Svert held it TRE. It was then assessed at 5 hides; now at 1 hide. When King William came into England, Vigot did not have it. There is land for 3 ploughs. This land belonged to Beddington. Villans held it. In demesne is now 1 plough; and 6 villans with 2 ploughs. TRE it was worth £4; afterwards 40*s.*; now 70*s.*

XXX. THE LAND OF HAMO THE SHERIFF

IN TANDRIDGE HUNDRED

● HAMO the sheriff holds TITSEY. Godtovi held it of King Edward. It was then assessed at 20 hides; now at 2 hides. There is land for 8 ploughs. In demesne are 4 ploughs; and 14 villans and 31 bordars with 5 ploughs. There is a church, and 9 slaves. For the pasture, the seventh pig of the villans. TRE it was worth £10; afterwards £6; now £11.

IN BRIXTON HUNDRED

● Hamo himself holds CAMBERWELL. Northmann held it of King Edward. It was then assessed at 12 hides; now at 6 hides and 1 virgate. There is land for 5 ploughs. In demesne are 2 [ploughs]; and 22 villans and 7 bordars with 6 ploughs. There is a church, and 63 acres of meadow, [and] woodland for 60 pigs. TRE it was worth £12; afterwards £6; now £14.

XXXI. THE LAND OF HUMPHREY THE CHAMBERLAIN

IN KINGSTON HUNDRED

● HUMPHREY the chamberlain holds of the queen's fief COOMBE. Alfred held it of the king, and could go where he would. It was then assessed at 3 hides; now at nothing. There is land for 2 ploughs. In demesne is 1 [plough]; and 3 villans and 4 bordars with 1 plough. There are 8 acres of meadow. TRE it was worth £4; afterwards 20*s.*; now 100*s.* TRW the woman who held this land put herself with it in the queen's hand.

XXXII. THE LAND OF RALPH DE FEUGERES

IN 'COPTHORNE' HUNDRED

● RALPH de Feugeres holds HEADLEY. Countess Gode held it of King Edward. It was then assessed at 7 hides; now at 2 hides and 1 virgate. There is land [. . .]. In demesne is 1 plough; and 9 villans and 5 bordars with 5 ploughs. There are 8 slaves, [and] woodland for 15 pigs. TRE it was worth £7; afterwards, as now, 100*s.*

IN WOTTON HUNDRED

● Ralph himself holds WESTCOTT. Abbot Æthelsige held it of King Edward. It was then assessed at 10 hides; now at 3 hides. There is land for 7 ploughs. In demesne is 1 plough; and 14 villans and 5 bordars with 7 ploughs. There are 3 slaves, and a mill rendering 30*d.*, and 2½ acres of meadow, [and] woodland for 30 pigs. TRE it was worth £9; afterwards, as now, £8.

XXXIII. THE LAND OF ALVRED OF MARLBOROUGH

IN WOKING HUNDRED

● ALVRED holds of the king SEND, and Reginald [holds] of him. Karli held it TRE. Then, as now, it was assessed at 20 hides. There is land for 10 ploughs. In demesne are 2 ploughs and 8 slaves; and 14 villans and 10 bordars with 6 ploughs. There is a mill rendering 21*s.* 6*d.* There is a church, and 5 fisheries rendering 54*d.*, and 100 acres of meadow, less 16, [and] woodland for 160 pigs.

Of this land, Walter holds 1½ hides, and Herbert 9 [hides] of the land of the villans. There are 2 ploughs in demesne, and 7 slaves, and 1 villan and 16 bordars. There is a mill rendering 2*s.* The whole TRE was worth £20; now the demesne [is worth] £10, and the rest 110*s.*

XXXIIII. THE LAND OF ALBERT

IN WALLINGTON HUNDRED

● ALBERT the clerk holds of the king ADDINGTON. Osweard held it of King Edward. It was then assessed at 8 hides; now at 2. There is land for 4 ploughs. In demesne are 2 ploughs; and 5 villans and 4 cottars with 1½ ploughs. [There is] woodland for 20 pigs. TRE, as now, [worth] 100*s.*

XXXV. THE LAND OF ODARD

IN 'ELMBRIDGE' HUNDRED

● ODARD the crossbowman holds of the king 4 hides in Esher. Tovi held them of King Edward. It is now assessed at 1 hide. There are 10 villans with 2 ploughs, and 2 acres of meadow. It is worth 40*s.*

● The same Odard holds [East or West] MOLESEY. Tovi held it of King Edward. It was then assessed at 6 hides and 1 virgate; now at 1 hide. There is land for 3 ploughs. In demesne is 1 [plough]; and 10 villans and 5 cottars with 4 ploughs. There is a church, and 2 slaves. TRE it was worth 100*s.*; afterwards 50*s.*; now £4.

XXXVI. THE LANDS OF OSWEALD AND OTHER THEGNS

IN EFFINGHAM HUNDRED

● OSWEALD holds of the king "PECHINGEORDE". He himself held it of King Edward. Then, as now, it was assessed at 1 hide. There is land for 3 ploughs. In demesne is 1 plough; and 3 villans and 2 bordars with 2 ploughs. There are 2 slaves. TRE and afterwards, as now, worth 40*s.* The men of the Bishop of Bayeux claim from this land every year for the king's use 2 marks of gold or 2 hawks, and this by grant of the abbot, brother to Osweald, namely for the battle which he ought to have fought against Geoffrey the Little.

● IN 'COPTHORNE' HUNDRED Sæmann holds 1 virgate of land which he held of King Edward. But from [the time] when King William came into England he has done service to Osweald, paying him 20*d.* This man could turn where he would TRE.

● Osweald himself holds FETCHAM. He himself held it of King Edward. It was then assessed at 11 hides; now at 3 hides. There is land [. . .]. In demesne is 1 plough; and 12 villans and 6 bordars with 5 ploughs. From a mill, 6*s.* 6*d.* There are 10 acres of meadow, [and] woodland for 4 pigs. TRE it was worth £4; now 100*s.*

IN WOTTON HUNDRED

● Osweald himself holds WOTTON. Harold held it TRE, but the men of the hundred say that they do not know how Harold had it. It was then assessed at 6 hides; now at 5 hides. There is land [. . .]. In demesne is 1 plough; and 20 villans and 7 bordars with 8½ ploughs. There is a mill rendering 20*d.*, and 3 acres of meadow. [There is] woodland for 50 pigs. From the herbage, 23 pigs. TRE, and afterwards, it was worth £8; now £7.

● Of these hides, [. . .] Richard of Tonbridge holds 1 hide, and Corbelin [holds] of him. Theodric held it of Harold as a manor. It was then assessed at 1 hide; now at half [a hide]. There is half a plough, and 2 villans and 1 slave. It was then worth 20*s.*; now 10*s.*

IN WOKING HUNDRED

● Osweald himself holds WISLEY. He himself held it of Earl Harold. It was then assessed at 3½ hides; now at 1½ hides. There is land for 2 ploughs. In demesne is 1 [plough]; and 4 villans and 4 bordars with 2 ploughs. There is a church, and 2 slaves, and a mill rendering 10*s.*, and 6 acres of meadow, and a fishery rendering 5*d.*, [and] woodland for 6 pigs. TRE it was worth 40*s.*; now 60*s.*

IN BRIXTON HUNDRED

● THEODRIC the goldsmith holds of the king KENNINGTON. He himself held it of King Edward. It was then assessed at 5 hides; now at 1 hide and 3 virgates. There is land for 2½ ploughs. In demesne is 1 plough; and 4 villans and 3 bordars with 2 ploughs. There is 1 slave, and 4 acres of meadow. It was and is worth £3.

IN WALLINGTON HUNDRED

● TEZELIN the cook holds of the king ADDINGTON. Godric held it of King Edward. It was then assessed at 8 hides; now at 1 hide. There is land for 4 ploughs. In demesne are 2 ploughs; and 8 villans and 9 cottars with 2½ ploughs. [There is] woodland for 20 pigs. It is and was worth 100*s.*

IN KINGSTON HUNDRED

● ANSGOT the interpreter holds of the king COOMBE. Cola held it TRE. It was then assessed at 3 hides; now at 1½ hides. There is land for 3 ploughs. In demesne is 1 [plough]; and 6 villans and 1 bordar with 1 plough, and 4 acres of meadow. For the herbage, 4 pigs. It is worth 60*s.*

IN WOKING HUNDRED

● KETIL the huntsman holds of the king [?]LOLLESWORTH. His father held it of King Edward. It was then assessed at 1 hide; now at half [a hide]. There is land for 2 ploughs. In demesne is 1 [plough]; and 2 villans and 5 bordars with 1 plough. [There is] a mill rendering 2*s.*, and 4 acres of meadow, [and] woodland for 20 pigs. It is and was worth 50*s.*

IN GODALMING HUNDRED

● WULFWIG the huntsman holds of the king LITTLETON. He himself held it of King Edward. Then [it was assessed at] 2 hides, but they did not pay geld; now at 1 virgate. There is land for 1 plough. There is [1 plough] in demesne; with 1 villan and 1 cottar with 1 plough. There are 2 acres of meadow. It is and was worth 20*s.*